The Divine Message About You

Sacred Teachings Supporting all Faiths
including the

Gentle Touch Practice

by
Robert Bourne

Naturally You
Publishing

United Kingdom

The Divine Message About You

Copyright © 2015 by Robert Bourne

2nd Edition

ISBN 978-0-9926644-7-3

Naturally You
Publishing

This book contains your Practice of
Gentle Touch for True Self Awakening

The Gentle Touch True-Self Awakening Practice
is available on Spotify and Apple Music
Search 'Gentle Touch Practice by Robert Bourne'

The New Awakening Process
contains nine multimedia modules

Gentle Touch Practice, Three Reiki Healing degrees,
Sacred Mantras, The Lotus Sutra, Sri Ramana Maharshi,
Awakening guidance by Sri Bhagavan, The Seekers Guide

for your free download visit
www.naturallyyou.co.uk
www.new-awakening.com

Contents

The Gentle Touch Practice

Autobiography

Introduction

There have been many books written by individuals who have reported conversations with God or clairvoyants who have received information channelled from other worldly spiritual beings communication. In most of these cases there is a sort of question and answer process between the separate person and the spiritual knower which results in guidance about specific things about life on this planet, life after death etc; all of these books are fascinating and are very helpful in leading us to take faith in some concept of a God.

The sacred teachings in 'The Divine Message About You' are different as they reveal the truth about who we really are. It is the right time in mankind's evolution for these truths to be revealed to everyone on the planet. It is these teachings that are at the core of every living being on the planet.

It is often said by many religions that The Truth will set you free. These eternal truths in a modern form have been revealed for this very purpose, to help set mankind free from the limitation and illusion about what the human race for thousands of years has collectively believed that we are.

When the 'I' drops back down from the mind into the oneness heart of Unconditional Love and Pure Awareness we are the God-self. It is this we have to awaken in place of our personal limited mind identity. It is not until a oneness of the human-being and the Pure, Divine, Eternal Being *(named God by many different faiths)* is established that mind illusion is removed. The good news is that this is within you right now.

The Divine Message About You

The thinking mind only identifies with life from its personal mind-body survival perspective seeing life only in separation; me and the other. From this understanding God is left out of the daily life creation process. The individual persons desires for happiness to be experienced becomes based upon a lessor mind consciousness and the personal struggle begins. Unshakable happiness, love, peace and contentment can only be found when you are resting within your heart centre.

The Gentle Touch Practice, the second half of this book, is about re-establishing Truth through direct experience. By awakening the Divine Love Presence as a direct experience we will eventually discover that we are all one with God and life will then be experienced in a very new way.

The key to transformation lies in surrendering all of what we think we know and connecting with God's Love. Our beliefs and knowledge are limited and in most peoples lives their mind is creating disharmony and therefore bringing about unsatisfied desire resulting in their unhappiness. It is our minds that require transformation from self-limiting beliefs and illusionary concepts about who we are.

The Gentle Touch Practice de-clutches the thinking mind allowing the True-self Divine Love Presence awakening to occur and illusion to be seen. When this happens a period of gentle transformation occurs by living life in a new way. Your transformation happens by staying with life's present moment awareness in the now, allowing the inner Divine Love Presence to transform that which is manifesting in your daily life experience. This creates a new freedom. God consciousness is now looking after your life!

Of course these sacred truths have to be believed in to give them full power. More importantly, a person reading these truths needs to personally realise them for themselves as the unique human being which they are. The purpose of providing a supporting 'Gentle Touch Practice' is for those who wish to directly experience an Awakening to Divine Love through the light of Pure Awareness.

The divine consciousness has presented you a bullet point statement of sacred truths about who we really are! There is no connection to any religion because the universal truths you will read in this book are the source of all religions.

You could say that this a new starting point. However the truth is that these sacred teachings are eternally present so they have always existed at the core of every one of us. They are the foundation source of all enlightenment throughout time. For example Christ was not a Christian, Buddha was not a Buddhist, Guru Nanak was not a Sikh. What did they awaken to? They were all enlightened to the same mind of God; the same eternal consciousness where there is only 'The One'.

I did not set out to create this set of divine truths or communicate with God; they just spontaneously became a direct knowingness within my mind. To give an example, using the analogy within the modern world, it would be the same as if a new software program was being installed on your computer.

The sacred teachings revealed themselves to me around December 2014 over several nights. I would go to bed about 11pm and then wake up feeling amazing, refreshed and full of life, with the room full of golden light, thinking that it was in the morning only to discover that it was only around 1am!

Then the download of the sacred teachings into my ordinary mind would start. My mind at the time was not thinking as it was completely still and at peace, it was in this golden state of pure awareness that I had all knowingness arise.

Looking at this a different way you could say I became one with what is eternally existing in relation to where mankind's evolution is today.

Having an understanding of how sudden inspirations and knowingness can disappear as quickly as they arrive, which happens as a result of the mind's consciousness falling into a lower state of awareness, I quickly got out my iPad rapidly typing away to capture what I had just received.

When the process had finished I started writing them up to create this new book to share with the world. The awareness then guided me to also create a spiritual practice which people could easily do to awaken these teachings within themselves.

A new form of Spiritual Community

After completing the new practice called 'Gentle Touch' the awareness then guided me to create a new form of spiritual community. A network of people throughout the world who wished to live their lives from unconditional love, living in the Divine presence of universal love.

The amazing thing about this new practice is that it is easy for anyone to do. Those who wish to run a group do not require any training. The only requirement is to download the 'New Awakening Process' and follow the teachings it contains.

When creating a New Awakening support community you do not have to run the groups, others you know may prefer to do this.

Some people prefer to hold groups others prefer to organise and support, a flexible approach is best. I am also happy for you to add this process to any groups that you may already run.

There are no Leaders or Organisation!

This is a new form of heartfelt support community whereby there are no leaders or organisation. It is the members who will be running the support groups themselves with no top-down control. All the New Awakening events are run by the members with love and compassion.

The core foundation Truth of Gentle Touch is that we are all spiritually enlightened now, therefore once we come together and connect to the oneness body of unconditional love, the pure light of awareness will guide us to flower uniquely.

The New Awakening objective is in creating as much value in society as possible through the development of people.

When people change through personally awakening to love, the world and the natural environment also change.

Download free the New Awakening Process today
Start a Support Group or open a Spiritual Community

www.naturallyyou.co.uk
www.new-awakening.com

The Divine Awakening Process

We are constantly in an ever changing process of evolution with all of existence. It is important to understand that you are enlightened now, however the two pure oneness bodies of 'Eternal Love' and 'Pure Awareness' are not normally fully shining in your life. You do however connect with them at times without realising that it has happened, but for most of the time they are laying dormant, just waiting for you to put your attention upon them; this is what the practice of Gentle Touch will do.

This means most people are blocking off two parts of themselves from being experienced. Therefore an adjustment to what you believe about yourself is initially required. In truth you are perfect now because you are these two bodies plus your own unique human body; the three create your true being self. These two pure bodies are regarded as oneness bodies because they are the same within everyone.

> The First belief to embrace - The two pure oneness bodies create an equality within the society of the world. They exist equally in everyone alongside the differences that each human being uniquely expresses.

> The Second belief to embrace is that you are connected to the two unchanging pure bodies. It is your body which they are trying to manifest through to enable you to have your unique human being existence.

It is these two pure bodies you are going to reconnect and open, through your practice of 'Gentle Touch'.

The first body of pure unchanging oneness consciousness is the body of pure awareness. This is male in nature and as such its light shines out throughout the whole of existence and is the light of pure awareness. It is this light which creates all of life. As it shines it creates form. As it slows down it changes into a waving form which becomes the second body of Love. As this light comes into the duality of life it creates all life forms. This light is the 'Gentle Touch' practice to reconnect you to inner contentment and stillness of mind, Pure Awareness.

The second Body of unchanging eternal love is connected to your heart through your emotional body. It is this energy which is very gently waving in form and is reflected inward, being feminine in nature. This is the 'Gentle Touch' energy practice to reconnect you back to the universal emotional body of love.

Three Stages of the Human Being's Evolution

The First Stage of evolution we all know and experience. It is living life as a separate person with a physical body containing an inner emotional and mental self awareness; the person tends to be guided by religion or just relies upon their own mind. At this stage we have free will which is limited to within our conditioned personality.

The Second Stage of evolution happens when the person realises that they are not separate from others in the world and become responsible for their own experiences, instead of blaming others for what happens to them. The person then enters upon a spiritual seeking journey to discover their higher or inner spiritual self; the person tends to choose their spiritual teachers instead of the religion they were born into, this can be the same.

The Third Stage of evolution happens when the person experiences that the divine and the unique human being are one; this is known as Mysticism. The conditioned person with its inherited genetic family tendencies of positive and negative are transformed and transcended into a state known as Awakening. In this state the person no longer exists and 'free will' is replaced with acceptance of the perfect ever changing moment in a blissful, joyful, loving all-knowing state of life; this is awakening into the enlightenment of being-ness.

We have Three Different Bodies

1. Physical Body (containing our emotions and mind): This body expresses our behaviour and will reveal where our consciousness is within the three stages of evolution. Where we are within the three stages of evolution determines the state of emotional life experience; whether it be suffering or contentment, joy, bliss or happiness.

2. Energy Body of Love: This acts as a bridge connecting our physical human selves to our pure Spiritual Formless Body. Many spiritual and healing practices or martial arts teach us how to connect and become aware of this comforting beautiful energy, which the person's mind can block and ignore.

3. Formless Spiritual Body: This is the unchanging pure source of all creation contained within all things. In religion it is known as God, in spiritual teachings it is known as our higher self and in Mysticism it is fully experienced and flows through our physical body.

The Nature of the Three Different Bodies

The First Body is the Physical Body (mind and emotions). We all know this with the mind's thinking, having very fast movements of thoughts. The various emotions that we feel through our everyday relationship experiences.

The Second Body is the Gentle Touch Energy Body. This energy moves at a slower rate and is pure in nature, it is the energy of love and healing. Therefore to become aware of this energy the mind and body has to slow down. For many people this is quite difficult but it is quite easily learnt or awakened in you through another awakened one who provides an attunement to this pure energy body. It is feminine in nature and transforms the emotional body, which is inward, into love. It is compassionate in nature and provides healing to the physical body.

There are many ways to experience this, such as healing, martial arts, tai chi etc. The problem that always emerges when this energy is first experienced is that the mind will require an explanation about what it is. Because of this, many explanations have been presented to us which become a sort of teaching to be believed in. Over history this multitude of various teachings and explanations have come about because of the different religions and cultures in the world. This has had the effect of giving the mind something to believe in which has caused a limitation to the true purpose of the energy body. Holding beliefs about this energy has had the effect of over complicating this connection and causing arguments about what it is.

The truth is that this energy is a bridge between our physical body and our still pure eternal self.

The Third Body is the Pure Eternal God Consciousness Body. This third body is in complete stillness. This body shines outwards so is creative or masculine in nature. This is where the concept of the light comes from. Therefore most people are never aware of this state of awareness because their minds are never still, because their mind is always thinking.

Having fully experienced pure stillness of the mind, experiencing life from a no thinking fully aware mind and the loving healing beauty of the Gentle Touch energy body, I realise that two approaches are required to share this experience with others, so that you can fully empower your life with all that is universally possible, enabling you to have the ability to express your unique human being-ness in daily life.

Learning to connect with the 'Gentle Touch' Energy body is the first step as this will bring comfort to you in the form of love to your emotions and healing to the physical body and mind. This will have the effect of slowing the mind, preparing it for the greater awareness of pure awareness stillness.

The Gentle Touch Energy Body will gently bring the qualities of the Pure Awareness body into your mind, body and emotions, freeing you from personal limitations, emotional suffering and limited mind-conditioned awareness.

Pure Awareness 'Gentle Touch' stillness practice is learnt to bring the body, mind and emotions together as a whole unit. A perfect alignment of the Physical body with the emotional pure body of love and the Pure Awareness body occurs. The three become integrated and become one unit working together.

Once this integration has occurred your life will become fully awakened and transformed into who you really are. You will become a living God! Just like all the enlightened masters we have known in our planet's history; Christ, Buddha, Mohammed, Guru Nanak, etc.

You have these three bodies exactly like these examples only you have not integrated them. You may have heard about the idea that 'being in the now' is important and that the future and the past are not alive but just memory or imaginations of the mind. Why do all enlightened beings make so much about this? Because of the teaching you have learnt about the three different bodies, it becomes very simple for the mind to grasp.

To live fully integrated in the three bodies you have to be in the moment, as it is the only place where complete stillness and alignment exists. Therefore learning stillness is the key to this experience known as enlightenment.

I hope you now understand and start to believe that you are enlightened now. The reason you don't fully experience this state of being is simply because you are just out of line with your three bodies and because you miss it and are running on conditioned programming - you start believing that is not possible for you.

When I say that you are enlightened now and that you are God, this is true once you align and integrate your three bodies. How could you be anything else? Right now you are God in potential like the caterpillar not yet transformed to the butterfly. 'Gentle Touch' accelerates the transformation process. You cannot escape this process of transformation. Many Masters say: "You are it. Just awaken to the God within you" and wonder why in three years time their followers are still asking the same questions from the person's mind state that they did when they first accepted this truth. Then a supernatural miracle approach is presented to help them make the leap. To me this only causes more separation as they enter into another relationship with their inner God and themselves. This has a wonderful place but what I am offering is a direct awakening with a process of transformation. The time is takes to transform you will vary according to the lifetimes the person has had plus their ancestral conditioning of the body they have inherited.

If your three bodies are disconnected or not aligned you remain a person trapped in the first body, just experiencing life through your physical, emotional and conditioned mind body.

Without awareness of your 'Gentle Touch' energy body or your Body of Pure Awareness you will believe you are a separate person living for survival in a jungle of other separate people all competing against each other for a larger share of the pie. It is this disconnection which causes you to feel isolated, experiencing suffering, emotional pain, the need for self protection, and self interest for survival. This person state of isolation is the cause of all the world's problems we experience on earth today.

In the light of Pure Awareness we are one. The light shines forth into this world and the whole of existence bathes in a sea of eternal love. The physical separate body is intended so we can meet each other as unique different human beings enabling us to dance and play together, bound together in a oneness body of love and compassion, being guided by the light of Pure Awareness in each single moment of our togetherness.

Key Points

- The Pure Awareness Body is one with all of life at the core all of existence.
- The loving Gentle Touch energy body is one and the same within all living beings.
- The physical body is separate and expressing life uniquely individually.

This explains that we are all connected together by love and pure awareness as one being, known as oneness but expressing its nature differently according our uniqueness.

The purpose of life is to enjoy the relationship of each other in the qualities of the two oneness bodies. It therefore is obvious that life cannot be enjoyed if we are not connected to our two oneness bodies.

Once this realignment occurs life is a dance of ever changing moment to moment love, bliss, contentment, peace and pure knowingness. When this is experienced sameness and uniqueness fully express themselves.

The natural world automatically supports us and is healed as it changes as we change in consciousness. This is like the analogy of the body and the shadow, wherein we are the body and as we move through changing our consciousness the shadow or environment follows.

Equality and Difference

The first belief to embrace: The two pure oneness bodies create an equality within every living being in the world. These two pure oneness bodies exist equally in everyone within the physical body which reveals the differences that each human being uniquely expresses.

Creating Inner Peace and Contentment

- The highest awareness in the whole of creation exists inside of you

- The highest awareness in the whole of creation exists equally in everyone else

- You are unique

- Everyone else is unique

- Everyone is different from each other

- Accept the differences between everyone

- Respect everyone as they are because they have the highest pure awareness inside of them

- Believe this truth and your life will flower into the unique human being you are meant to be

- We are one being displaying different unique aspects

Three Understandings
to
Liberate Your Life

There are three key things you need to know that are the main causes for preventing your pure bodies from freely flowing into your life. Understanding these three key points will bring a new opportunity for you to change your attitude, belief and thinking in your life. This will have the effect of aligning your beliefs and thinking with the truth of the universal mind of pure consciousness.

Just by changing your beliefs and knowing these three truths you will automatically align your personal conditioned mind to the pure body of Pure Awareness and your emotional body to the body of Pure Love.

What happens when you do this is that you are now ready to activate these two bodies when you practice the 'Gentle Touch' practice without any internal resistance held by illusions and past hurts stored in your limited computer mind. When you practice Gentle Touch it will immediately clear the internal memory of its negative patterning program, which has been causing you limitations and suffering in your life, without any effort or probing around any of your life's problems.

Key Points

The first understanding is that any problems in your relationship with your Mother will cause problems in your relationships with other people.

The second understanding is that any problems with your relationship with your Father will cause you problems in your material life, such as work money and possessions.

The third understanding is that any problems of guilt or personal identity about your sexuality can prevent your connection to pure awareness and pure love to become blocked.

I would like to give some known examples about these three understandings with explanations as to why I am saying they hold the key to your liberation.

Tantric Yoga uses sexual union as a practice to fully activate the pineal and pituitary glands in the brain to cause the awakening of the inner dormant state of enlightenment within the mind. This method is used and known in some Indian Tantra and Taoist practices. This is about the kundalini/pineal gland activation spiritual awakening. It is therefore crucial to be free from guilt in relation to orgasm.

Having read many eastern explanations of the three bodies, although practices may vary, there is a common agreement that the human body is connected to the spiritual enlightened body by the energy body known as chi or prana. This is fantastic news because this chi energy body is so easily accessed by anyone who wishes to experience it. The chi body is connected to in the 'Gentle Touch' practice. This Universal Love Energy is the basis for all meditation and enlightenment. The practice of 'Gentle Touch' has been created precisely for this purpose.

The good thing is that no faith, religion or spiritual practice is required to practice it. In fact it will enhance any belief you may already have. If in doubt ask your religious or spiritual leader if they object to you experiencing more love in your life, developing a clear and still mind so you are able to experience life in the present moment with perfect clarity, being held and comforted by a loving guiding energy. How can they say no? They might secretly wonder how you can achieve this, which is a state reserved for saints and enlightened masters!

Unfortunately in western society it is based upon science and neuroscience. Alone their methodology is unable to access this energy connection because it is not of the mind, because it is emotion of the Universal Love Energy. This energy is then left to be explained and experienced through faith, religions and spiritual practices.

This leads onto three very important solutions to personal suffering which are caused by not understanding the main reasons that block the person from connection with their two pure bodies. I have written another book that goes into this more deeply The Seekers Guide for a New Awakening - Robert Bourne ISBN: 978-0-9561159-7-3

Three Key Points

The first point to learn is that it is important to understand that the Universal Body of Love is inward and feminine in nature. It is represented as our Mother.

The second point is that the body of Pure Awareness flows outward and creates existence and is masculine in nature. This is represented as our Father.

The third point to learn is that our sexual energy is the source of our awakening in the brain connecting the two pure bodies of love and awareness.

Our body is not our body, it is the combination of our Mother and Father through sexual union. Any problems or issues with our Mother or our Father or our sexuality are reflected in our daily life more than we realise. For example our relationship problems can be the result of problems with the Mother, and work and material accomplishment can be the result of problems or issues with the Father. Problems with our sexuality generally keep us locked into our conditioned self and can prevent awakening from occurring. This produces inner guilt, inner conflict and emotional suffering.

When you see that your physical Mother and Father are just a reflection of the two pure bodies you have incarnated inside of you, your attitude needs to change. Change your attitude to acceptance of your Mother and Father with deep appreciation for giving you life.

You may say that you have been mistreated by your parents, or they have abandoned you, or that you have not been supported by them. For these reasons you say that they are not nice people. Society will do everything it can to support this truth, however for you to experience liberation from this hurt a new approach needs to be taken. This solution I am offering is the fast track to freedom from personal suffering and ancestral conditioning.

- I am saying yes, what your parents are is most probably true therefore the first thing to do is accept their suffering and limitations.

- Now give thanks to your parents for giving you life. Because of this life you have the opportunity to become free from the negative conditioning and programs you have inherited and awaken to your two pure bodies of Love and Awareness.

- When you see you Mother as an energy which represents the pure body of Love, to reject that energy rejects all female energy. This is why it causes problems within relationships.

- When you see your Father as an energy which represents the pure body of Awareness, to reject that energy will cause you problems in your daily life with your career and finances.

The Divine Message About You

Knowing this it becomes even more important to accept these truths. Then the inner pure bodies will react accordingly. Remember the pure male and female aspects of Love and Wisdom are waiting to guide you. They are waiting to flow through your body so that you will flower into the unique human being that you are meant to be; not the conditioned programmed person you have inherited from your ancestors. The other side of this coin is that not all of your conditioning is negative, therefore gratitude towards all your ancestors, including your parents is required for the positive aspects that are naturally within you.

Regarding your sexual gender, again you are a mix of both male and female aspects. These two beautiful energies combine and create a unique expression for your relationships with others, especially on an intimate sexual basis.

I know many people who struggle with being in a male or female body as they express the opposite inner sexual energy or both equally. We do not fit into a certain box. We are all unique combinations of male and female energy.

There is a lot of conditioning about this issue which is limiting and therefore not the truth. Regarding your liberation or your enlightenment and contentment just embrace the attitude of knowing this truth and embrace everyone with acceptance, without questioning. Having this attitude will accelerate your freedom when you carry out your daily practice of 'Gentle Touch'.

Ancestors
Friends and Family who have died

- You never die, life is always changing and evolving

- Upon the death of your physical body your mind/soul continues to live

- Without your knowing, some family and friends are still connected to you and are still influencing your life choices

- This proves that your body is a vehicle gifted to you for you to live and experience your life.

- The body contains behaviour conditioning known as programs; many of these were created by your family ancestors and not you

- Some inherited conditioning and programs in the body are positive and some are negative

- The body you have now is a gift from your family; your ancestors - be grateful to them for your life opportunity

- Having a physical body gives you the gift of having the power to change anything in your life's mind/soul

- When your ancestors die they are still connected to you through your body and mind/soul

- When you change to a higher awareness you can 'Liberate Your Ancestors', your dead family and friends. This is achieved through your daily practice of 'Gentle Touch'

- When you change or switch off the negative programs you pass this on to your deceased family and friends, this is known as mind-body-soul evolution

Clearing a Nation's Negative Karma

Sri Bhagavan

- The best way is to ask forgiveness of your ancestors

The Purpose of Life

The purpose of life is to live. There cannot be any purpose. But what does this mean? The practice of 'Gentle Touch' is to help you to live. You most probably are not living now. You think you are alive but in a sense you are dead to the full potential that you really are.

Only when you become awakened do you really start living, until then you do not know what it is to live. So why or how did you come away from the light? The light created the separation so we can start playing and enjoy our existence. The problem is that no one appears to be playing because everyone has become serious.

The solution is for you to become awakened as a direct experience then you will know the contrast, the difference between a separated life from your two pure spiritual bodies. When you are once again fully connected you will be living in fullness and completeness.

Separation is empty with a constant struggle with yourself and others. Oneness is the integration of your three bodies. This state creates a life of play, of love, of dance, of completeness, totally happy and content, this is being alive and living your true potential effortlessly.

Freedom from Guilt

It is important to realise that nobody is responsible for what we are. In a society where the collective consciousness is low there is blaming and judgement about those unfortunate people who appear negative and who are behaving in a negative way.

Once you stop slandering and putting down others who behave negatively you stop adding to negative low consciousness. Yes, just by putting others down who are less fortunate than ourselves you add to a lower state of consciousness, causing even more negative behaviour to appear in every day life.

When the level of consciousness rises then the by-product within society is that unwanted behaviour changes and even stops completely. The way to raise consciousness is with your own life condition. This is the purpose of your daily practice of 'Gentle Touch'. It is very liberating to know that in just changing yourself you affect everyone in the world in a positive way.

The reason for this is that we are all one. We are living in a collective consciousness whereby different people live out different parts according to the collective consciousness we have all created.

This explains that the most important contribution to mankind you can make is to change yourself. One great step is to stop judging others and accept that what is here and happening is perfect.

The Divine Message About You

It is judgement that is causing all the problems. This is the result of your mind being the communicator which causes noise. Once you develop the pure awareness state of mind you are communicating in the divine consciousness of silence, which is transformational upon society.

Dropping all Concepts and Beliefs

What prevents awakening from happening is that mankind's mind has been filled by too many ideas and different beliefs about life. Once you can empty yourself of everything you think you know and believe in, Awakening and Enlightenment is naturally there.

Continue to practice daily your 'Gentle Touch' to clear your mind of all beliefs. This is where attending a group will help by receiving Love from another as the power in the room is amplified by the square root of the number of people attending a share. Awakening will happen naturally, very fast, and all by itself.

I remember that my own awakening came about because of saying that whatever I think I know is limited and in truth I don't know if anything I believe in is true. I then had a direct experience of unconditional love and pure silence. My person dissolved and I have lived in a state of mind where there is no thinking, an inner mind silence without trying. For many years I attended development group meetings where everyone was having experiences except me. I always had the same no thinking mind of silence. Only recently have I fully realised what had happened to me.

The Mind, Beliefs and Imagination

Without the imagination there would be no horror! The personal mind of the body tends to work in an earth bound past, present and future basis. This is what gives us the idea that life is linear and is set upon some time line. When this mind has aligned itself with the mind of Pure Awareness then only the present moment exists. This is known as living in the now. Most people's suffering comes from emotional and mental torture as a result of having experienced past negative experiences. How many people are unable to have positive loving relationships because of past hurt? How many people are unable to trust others because of past betrayal or deception? This personal mind is protecting you to its best ability but is unable to do anything more than create limitations for you to live your life from. Building protective barriers is all well and good but they prevent you from living in love and contentment; you are handicapped from living your life to the full potential.

Aligning your three bodies will protect you by moving your mind into contentment, confidence of living, blissful joy with the gift of knowingness or universal wisdom. This gives you the confidence to know you will always make the right choice for your life in every single moment of it.

To help you live in the now a very powerful teaching for you to practice is this. Whenever you are feeling past pain of a bad experience become aware that 'It is not happening now' but only in your memory. Because your Pure Awareness body does not know time it creates anything you ask it to create, so it creates the memory again for you, hence the painful emotional experience is re-experienced.

Help Practice: Catch your mind dwelling on a problem or past trauma and ask yourself "Is this Happening Now?" Then snap yourself back into what is happening now and you then say "This is not happening now - so it is over."

Beliefs are one of the most difficult to overcome as they are lodged in the deepest part of the computer mind. What tends to happen is you are having a daily life experience and to make meaning of it you revert back into the computer mind to find out if you have anything there that relates to what you are experiencing. Then the beliefs will come forward to judge what is happening, turning your experience into good or bad. This disconnects your life from your pure bodies of Love and Awareness and causes unpleasant emotions of agreement or disagreement, anger or rapture to be experienced in the emotional body. To go a step further you may then take some action according to your reaction to what you have encountered. All of this is based upon illusion caused by the beliefs that you hold.

How to deal with this is very simple - acceptance of what is happening. To accept, although you may not understand at the time of the experience, will realign you to your two pure bodies of Love and Awareness. In time as you continue to live life by accepting what is happening without interpretation, higher awareness will naturally arise and you will intuitively without thinking gain an understanding of the perfection of what is happening.

Help Practice: Accept what is happening as perfect. Drop all interpretations about everything and accept that your knowledge is limited. Understand that your beliefs have come from what others have taught you or are ancestral inheritance and may not be the Truth of 'What is'.

By doing this together with your daily practice of 'Gentle Touch' you will speed up the transformation process for your total alignment of your three bodies. In truth the two pure bodies are already in harmony and aligned together; it is your physical body that needs to come into alignment with them.

Help Practice: This is where surrender of our limited mind's conditioning to the universal knowingness of Pure Awareness is practiced. It makes sense to create a space in our mind, to quiet and slow down our mind so that the inner silence and contentment comes forth. The Deeksha energy transfer from Awakened beings or 'Awakening Trainers', our spiritual guides will also accelerate this process together with your daily practice of 'Gentle Touch'.

Wealth Consciousness

"What is meant by wealth consciousness is not just about money. For example your parents are wealth, your children are wealth, your husband or wife or partner is wealth, your house is wealth, all that you have is wealth and you become aware of that.

It is just like the practice of gratitude. This you must do on an individual basis. By doing this you are developing wealth consciousness which causes the inner pure consciousness to create more of what you have or what you desire.

Understanding this is a very powerful practice to obtaining inner contentment. Doing this in conjunction with 'Gentle Touch' practice will create miracles.

As you develop wealth consciousness this will also have a positive effect on your family and country which will cause a positive change in society." *Sri Bhagavan*

The Difference Between Awakening and Enlightenment

Question:

What is the difference between Awakening and Enlightenment?

Sri Bhagavan's Answer:

- Awakening is when you can stay with the 'What Is' without effort. This refers to the level of awareness. How aware you are determines the amount of changes that have happened in the brain. This is why Awareness is referred to as a journey to awakening.

- Enlightenment is when all day dreaming has stopped.

- Transformation is the flowering of the heart where you no longer see yourself separate from the other.

- Complete transformation is the disappearance of the self, the senses getting disjointed and the self is gone, being replaced with the pure presence of unconditional love.

- Transformation happens very easily when you experience the suffering of others and start helping them.

Pure Awareness
The First Pure Body
'Gentle Touch' Practice connects with this Pure Body

The Vital Source

The Light of Pure Awareness comes from the formless unchanging aspect of all of existence described as God, Universal field, The Void etc. I call all previous reference to God etc. the Vital Force because there are mind references for this term. If I mention God many will start arguing about what God is. The vital source now can take on the meaning you give it. Its name suggests it is the life giving centre of you and me and all that is in creation. It is Pure Consciousness, Pure Awareness coming from the light of truth.

When you lose your limited mind your limited personal mind is exchanged for your natural mind and everything flows in perfect harmony. Your life is just put before you and this happens automatically. This mind is known as the awakened mind, being awakened and living in the presence of love is this experience.

Pure Awareness Practice

- Dropping all of what you think you are

- Accepting yourself exactly as you are

- Accepting that you can never be understood as the unique being that you are. This relates to personality, body mind aspect. Because of the two oneness bodies we are the same as everyone.

Doing this allows the alignment to reoccur with your pure body of Pure Awareness. When a connection is made to Pure Awareness this stimulates your true energy emotional body of Love to be experienced. This unchanging pure body is common to all living beings. This is why we are never alone and can have love for everyone.

The enjoyment of the other then emerges in appreciation for their unique expression or flowering of Love.

Connection with this oneness body of love is achieved through the practice of 'Gentle Touch'.

Deep within you, at your very core, the centre of your uniqueness is in total stillness of the universal mind. In your third eye you may see the light that never goes out, the eternal flame within all of life. In fact it is life before Love. It shines from nothingness outwards hence it is the creator of all that is. It is untouchable hence it is constant. It is this which created you, me and everything.

Pure awareness practice is simply re-connecting to this eternal light to create a stillness unmoving mind of pure contentment and peace.

You become the creator without needing to desire anything because everything you need is put before you effortlessly. In religion it would be said you have inherited the Kingdom of God. All our past prophets, our past enlightened gurus have awoken to this truth. It is at this point of stillness that the thinking mind stops and the questioner disappears. In its place arises the contentment of not knowing, however when required in the moment, the wisdom of the external now arises to guide your choice making in the moment. The external light is the knowingness of all that is.

From this state of centred stillness or emptiness of mind everything is perfect as it is. This perfection is experienced in its many different expressions of lower consciousness which are constantly moving. From this state there is no duality, although duality of cause and effect still exist.

It is in the stillness of being that you experience the golden coming together of cause and effect so that the moment is expressing cause and effect at the same time. This is living beyond the person's conditioning, beyond the personal mind which is in constant movement.

Living from the personal mind is what causes problems and creates trouble as it is always reflecting upon known memory before taking action to live your life. It is this thinking mind that draws upon and misuses your creativity to project some future security, wherein one day everything is going to be alright.

It is this mind that knows nothing about the perfection of the now, because it exists outside of what it is! You could describe it as a computer calculating machine, which only knows what has been experienced or learnt and borrowed from others.

If you are to live in freedom and express the beautiful unique human being that you are you have to place your attention upon that which is at your very core right now.

Only when your awareness becomes still are you experiencing the core of your pure awareness, unfiltered, non restricted by ideas and concepts about life. It is then you experience causeless joy and bliss of the golden perfection of all there is!

The intended purpose of all Meditation is to arrive at this experience

- You are the peace in silence
- You are the silence in peace
- You are the light of consciousness that causes all things to be seen
- You are the perceiving love devoid of objective identity
- You are the wisdom and love which shines from the source of existence
- You are Unborn Awareness Self

~ Mooji

To clarify this statement I understand the Oneness of True Self to be known as We instead of You. This is because the two pure oneness bodies of Love and Pure Awareness are the incarnated same in all life forms within the whole of creation. It is the uniqueness of our human being which is the You - the I being expressed in total alignment with the two bodies; this is enlightenment. The conditioned person is no longer there, however uniqueness still exists. Suffering or lower consciousness is known as the mind ego, a state of existence out of alignment with the two pure bodies of Love and Pure Awareness.

A lot is made of spiritual practices to cause transformation of the mind's ego but all you need to know is the truth that you are it now and return to stillness; expressing love for all mankind and existence will naturally follow.

I have included a mantra used in healing called Cho Ku Rei. A full explanation will be given in the essential practice technique section. This mantra has a symbol which describes the light coming from pure awareness through our crown chakra into the perfect moment. This energy is rising up through our rainbow body through the seven energy chakras from our feet. This happens in a spiral which is represented in the symbol. This creates the physical body to enable the two pure bodies of Love and the Light of pure Awareness to be experienced in this world as a love play.

Most people are not aware and have been conditioned to believe they are separate individuals without spiritual pure bodies. This causes the blocking off from pure awareness which reverts the person to become reliant upon the lifetimes of memory including ancestral memory stored within the limited personal mind. The emotional body is now restricted and separated from pure limitless love and becomes dependent upon a person's love experience coming from another person, instead of being in a constant state of love, which is not dependent upon a single person.

I have repeated this truth several times because I want you get the concept even if you have not yet experienced it. Once you can have a realisation that this is a truth you will be able to transform any previous illusionary beliefs that your mind is holding your life as the prisoner of conditioning. This is a get out of jail card.

As you carry out your daily practice of 'Gentle Touch with the simple belief that YOU ARE pure love and pure awareness, although currently your conditioning is blocking you off from fully experiencing this integration, you will discover a very quick transformation taking place in your life. Very soon you will awaken to, and be living in the presence of love as a daily life experience.

You are the light of all understanding. The light comes from within you at your very core. The very fact that you can communicate in some way proves this to be true.

There have been a lot of teachings which go into great detail to explain the experiences we have in life and what we are to do with them, but all this misses the very important point that it is this Pure Awareness, the light that is always there within all things but always missed. It is missed because it can't be this simple. The mind wants something fantastically distorted away from reality with fireworks and all those supernatural bells and whistles.

To fully experience this unchanging eternal light of truth and understanding first of all requires an openness in your attitude, in your approach to fully experiencing the joy that spontaneously arises when you are one with this pure body of awareness that is at the core of all within creation.

The difficulty comes in the way we experience the manifest creation that we see before us. This apparent reality is unstable in nature because it is always changing and once we know what something is it becomes stored within our computer mind memory, thinking that it is fixed and permanent.

One of the mind's beautiful functions is to help us identify with what we are experiencing, what is happening in our lives. The object we meet is identified along with our past emotional relationship identification. The computer mind is trying to be helpful by protecting our life at a basic survival level of living.

We know that living in this way causes a tendency of life being divided into two categories nice or good and unpleasant and bad. This is fine as a basic level of life where you need to survive and reproduce as a separate person who is living in competition with all other people on this planet.

You are reading this because you are looking for more than the limitation of separation with the loneliness that it brings with it.

Yes, you are looking for more, for freedom to discover contentment and love therefore it is essential to be able to recognise this way of thinking and living. Once you do this you can approach your moment to moment experience in a new way. This is what to do.

Key Points

- Whatever is happening you need to stay in the moment and just observe it.

- You need to first of all discover if it is really happening or if your computer mind is distorting the real truth of the moment by bringing a past memory to the situation and hence distorting it and turning the experience into something positive or negative.

- Remember you are enlightened now and if you can see the present moment from your Pure Awareness without filtering it through your computer mind then a Beauty will arise as you will be seeing the truth from your highest consciousness. The light of truth of all knowingness is shining out of you all the time.

With this understanding you will start transforming your past hurts and memory into happiness and joy. You will set yourself free from your limitations and computer memory. Of course it will all still be there but the emotional effect on you will not be there. You will be free form suffering because you will be living in the now of Pure Awareness. This is pure seeing from the eyes of what has been called God. This is enlightenment.

The thing to be aware of, which can cause people to say this is not true, is the issue of the time for transformation of your soul, of your mind and lifetimes memory. This also brings in your inherited conditioning from your ancestors and the genetics within your body. It is this which has created a memory program that is running automatically in your life. This explains why we feel trapped and are unable to free ourselves from these limitations. This program has positive and negative aspects. It also has a certain consciousness to it which means you will be vibrating in a certain frequency of consciousness. Your objective is to realign yourself to your Body of Pure Awareness and live from the stillness experienced from your very core.

The light of Truth will then shine in the present moment transforming the past which is being put before you now. Yes, your current life moment when living as a person from your conditioned memory is a past event trying to be set free and transformed in the light of your core truth which is shining upon it. This is why the guidance of living with the 'What is in the present moment' is so often used but no one has really taken the time to explain why it is so important.

When you do this the conditioning may be very strong, so this is where your 'Gentle Touch' practice will rescue you. It will anchor you in the present moment emotionally with the emotion of Love energy; any pain or past suffering will now be dissolved. The divine Mother of compassion and healing will bless you, liberating you from your suffering. This is the place all miracles happen. It is all within you. The other energy of pure awareness will anchor you in the present moment, for this light of transformation will bring bliss, joy and contentment to your experience.

This practice transforms the past memories and patterns not only for you but for your ancestors as well. This is how you liberate your ancestors. This is how you liberate others on the planets who have a connection with the same issues.

How beautiful for you to know that through changing yourself you are also helping so many others. This happens because we all draw upon the collective thoughts and memories from mankind's existence. You transform that which is flowing within you and you enlighten and free yourself from its bondage.

How long this takes depends upon the unique individual. Do not be concerned about this but you rest in the assurance that it is taking place. The time will come when this program has been completely dissolved.

When this occurs Awakening arrives whereby you have aligned your emotional body to the body of Love and you live from the presence of love which guides your daily life. Your Pure Awareness body now transforms the illusion of ideas and concepts in the thinking mind into the pure truth of eternal knowingness. In this state enlightenment occurs naturally. This is very beautiful.

It is this state of awakening to the presence of love when you allow love to run your life. You go into automatic pilot whereby your uniqueness can flower into daily life without effort or the need to plan or strategise your future. This point changes from the limited mind running your life giving you choices based upon past knowledge, to living from no choice and having everything you need put before you for your happiness. This change in living only comes about once the transformation of your mind conditioned program has occurred.

In truth this state is what masters refer to as 'no person there'! They are referring to the limited conditioned separated self which in truth is just a collection of past memory experiences.

Mooji

I wish to quote Mooji who eloquently explains this very important truth, the fact that you are already the truth, that you are already enlightened.

"The light of understanding dispels the darkness and this is already within you. There is a joy which arises when this light hits its mark and dispels the darkness of ignorance. It cannot give you the light because the light is already present within you.

You are here, what more can you say? Whatever you describe will only be another phenomenal thing. We know that all phenomenal manifestations are impermanent by nature. Something inside of you knows not to pursue that, don't get involved or stuck into any of that because it is not reliable. Moods are changing, feelings are changing, thoughts are changing, identity is changing.

Everything is changing, everything just comes and goes. Has anything ever changed? No, it comes and goes but when we have a particular fascination for a thing it is as though you give it longevity, you give it life which it doesn't naturally have. We impart life to it because that life arises from your own aliveness, your own sentient-ness, it gives life or apparent life to even inanimate things. Such is your power. It is largely unrecognised - we are still naive about ourselves.

44

When you discover what actually is, your mind cannot argue with it. This is the purpose of staying with the What Is. This is not a promise about the future, this is about showing you what is here now. The mind is the instrument of comparing, of measuring, of interpreting, but how can it evaluate that which is formless? Where is the location of that which is perceiving inside and outside simultaneously, where is its location?"

Mooji explains - "That which goes out and comes back, which presently you are referring to you as yourself, is not yourself it is your ATTENTION. It is the idea you have of who you are, it is your self image that goes out and comes back. When it returns to you it is happy, it is complete. When it goes out, an energy goes with it, an energy goes with it, an identity goes with it, it has the power to create a secondary identity and reality and that is what we are taking to be our self.

Your real self is that which is here. It looks like it is behind this secondary identity, the ego self. Your true self does not know behind or in front it is so pure, it just Is! Behind and in front happen in the realm of consciousness of the mind, the dynamic consciousness which is always changing.

There is only consciousness. Even the ego is consciousness, however it is consciousness which is severely limited by identifying with the limited body and obviously the limited conditioning. It is residing in a narrower or lower state of consciousness. Because of that it embraces the limitation, as a part of what it is and believes that to be real.

What gives the person the sense of reality? The feel of reality is the vital force and the fact that consciousness is always there. This makes the ego feel real because it is also consciousness. Much of its reality is a construction of changeful or impermanent elements. It is afraid of those elements because it cannot keep them to be permanent because they keep changing and dying. Every time something dies off which is natural for that thing because the consciousness associates and identifies with that thing, it feels the pain. Oh this is going, it is dying, but it is only natural for it to go. You must find the thing that cannot go!"

To understand anything in these teachings you don't understand you have to go over and over it again until it awakens within you. This is the purpose of learning the 'Gentle Touch' loving energy connection because it will become a bridge between the limited mind and body and the pure truth of your core being.

This transforms you by dissolving the limited understanding to awaken the inner eternal light of truth within your being. You will return home to your core. You will know when this happens because you feel a freedom like a space opening up. Then you have got it. You will know you have got it because you become so totally content, so totally present, life becomes very sweet in this space of freedom from the conditioned and limited personality.

What is God-Infinite Being?

Awakening Your True Potential

- The truth is everything is Infinite Being!

- This means you, your friends and family, in fact every living being is God.

- You will probably have a lot to say about this. I would be very surprised if you didn't.

- The Ultimate Truth is that You are God/Infinite Being!

- Life comes into existence from a formless God/Infinite Being.

- The physical, mental and emotional You is the ever changing part of the pure, loving, all knowing, formless, eternal, unchanging inner you, which is God; the two aspects make the total God!

- The daily experience you have in your life plus the condition of the natural environment, nature, depends upon how you create your life experience.

- This is because you are the creator God-Infinite Being!

- For example, what you are now inside of you is what you get. What you believe about yourself is what you get back to you from the outside, others in the world.

- This inner conditioning you carry affects everything in the world, not just people and animals but the natural world, trees flowers, water, rocks, air etc.

- Why? Because you are God the creator!

- Believe, think and feel poverty and yes you get and experience poverty!

- Feel, think and be abundance and yes you get and experience an abundant life!

- For example I am not rich, in fact I am considered poor, but I live in abundance and always get what I want! I live in total contentment, inner Love and Happiness. Because I am God-Infinite Being I receive contentment, love and happiness.

- You are not able to just think this, you have to become this on the inside!

- Many questions will come now if you are living or vibrating from the first or second stage in evolution out of the total three stages of evolution.

- To learn more about this start with 'Creating Abundance' contained in 'The Seeker Guide' because you need to understand this to be able to change where you are now. The question is, "Who wrote the Program?"

Relationships and Love

'Gentle Touch' will help awaken and transform the heart into a deeper awareness   and most importantly a direct experience of universal love. Once this is experienced you will notice a profound transformation in yourself where it will affect the way you relate to others on a personal level.

After a short while you will not be the same person you are now in so many ways. You will have a profound effect upon how you relate to other people, on the way you communicate with other people without making any effort or trying to be different, it will be natural, without making any effort. This is a very beautiful transformation.

'Gentle Touch' is Pure Love

Gentle Touch is common and within all forms of life. What is it?   It is the connecting or bridging energy between the unchanging Pure Awareness body and the moment to moment ever changing physical body of the Human Being.

Every living being on the planet knows very well about the physical body which allows us to experience our daily lives. Mankind has become extremely aware through scientific discovery as to how this body works.

The life giving unchanging aspect of life, which gives life to all that is, has only been known throughout history by a few enlightened human beings on our planet.   These handful of human beings have left a message through their lives which has displayed beautiful behaviour in terms of love and compassion towards all of life. They have displayed a profound wisdom towards life and the whole of existence having within them an ability to magically heal others, providing life changing experiences to those who come into contact directly with them.

These special beings have left mankind a memory of their living proof of what the human being is capable of being. You too can have this experience once the human body is directly connected to the Pure body of its creation.

Today we are seeing the early stages of mankind awakening to a new evolutionary phase in our known history. We are seeing many people living in a new way, whereby they have awakened to the third stage of our evolution through becoming directly conscious of the Pure unchanging eternal body.

Relationships
Love and Suffering

- Love is always trying to emerge between all people, in fact it is your natural state

- When two people experience this love, a form of overwhelming occurs

- Each person will feel a sort of losing it

- Two people decide they both want to experience more of this emerging

- It is natural for a person to regain control to set rules and conditions wherein this love is allowed to be expressed

- Love knows no rules or limitations it just knows love through total acceptance

- Suffering occurs when the agreed rules are broken

- Two reactions are typical, expression of hurt towards the other, expression of hurt towards oneself

- To become free from suffering first recognise that any projected nasty words or behaviour are purely an expression of pain in the other or you

- You are not that which they say you are, therefore allow them to express their pain without reaction!

The Divine Message About You

- Total freedom from emotional suffering is experienced when you become the love you experienced from another without them being there!

- The Love you seek is seeking you all the time because it is at the centre of your heart

- This Universal Love is the Divine Mother. Ask her to comfort you when you are suffering and she will

- Ask her to feed you love and it will be given

- Ask her to open your heart and it will be opened

- Ask the inner Divine Mother of Universal Love to heal you and she will. This is the source of all miracles and this source is always within you, eternally

- The key to this transformation is in your surrender, Om Namo - Namaha (to bow)

- To accelerate your experience of Love, give love to the Divine Mother because Love attracts Love, Become Love and you will only experience Love in all things

Sex and Relationships

- Personal emotional security is the secret to fulfilling relationships

- When you are dependent upon another for your fulfilment and happiness you are emotionally vulnerable

- It is a beautiful thing to enjoy the experience of being in love with another

- To enhance your relationships emotional security is required, this is only achieved by a connection to inner love

- When you feel love then acceptance of the other is automatic

- No matter what they do you will not be threatened or project their behaviour upon yourself believing you are the cause of them being the way that they are

- The inner love connection achieved through the practice of Gentle Touch will bring emotional security to your life and the creation of happy relationships

Personal issues in relation to orgasm often are related to childhood conditioning. Discovering that masturbation creates a beautiful emotional experience of orgasm is often in conflict with what parents or teachers have warned you about having sex. This is of course based upon their concern for the young child or teenager about the possibility of them getting pregnant in the case of a girl or in the case of a young boy fathering a child.

Many people suffer from conflicts with having an orgasm, brought about by themselves or within a relationship. The conflict is in the fact that the orgasm is a beautiful experience, bringing a lot of pleasure to the body. Having been told not to do this, for whatever reason, creates an emotional conflict causing the person to have emotional feelings of guilt and even self hatred etc.

The truth is once you have emotionally entered into a relationship, intimacy is required to maintain a natural exchange of love. It is this area of relationship where the orgasm is required to be accepted for the truth of what it is. When the heart is open orgasm is required to take the experience of sex to the experience of pure universal love and Bliss.

The sex drive is a life inbuilt program to maintain the continuation of the species. An orgasm is therefore natural and in a human form the coming together of the three spiritual bodies in one moment of creation. To deny or repress this as unclean, bad, dirty etc. is to repress your emotional inner life of Love. This causes all sorts of problems of intimacy within human relationships.

Accept orgasm as being natural and experience this from love. The experience then becomes very blissful with your partner, if you both approach sex from love. Use your practice of 'Gentle Touch' to share love with another in order to experience something greater than the personal orgasm. This is the subject of Tantra.

Basically the woman's element is like water which needs to become warm before sex takes place, this is why often there is the requirement of loving foreplay 'Gentle Touch'.

The male tendency or element is that of fire which bypasses the heart coming straight from the mind, having been stimulated by the woman's bodily form or sexual images, causing sexual excitement. The tendency for the male then is to get carried away by passion or lust wanting only to penetrate and ejaculate. The male sexual drive is just nature's need to procreate. Men who are only rooted in their human body have a tendency to get overwhelmed for the need to have sex, without the consideration if the women is receptive to receive him at that time for the sexual act.

To fully overcome conditioning about sex being negative, a strong, inner security is required in both partners. This is achieved through the practice of 'Gentle Touch' to develop inner love in themselves first.

The other requirement is to accept that sex is natural and very beautiful, it is creation itself in play; at the highest level of consciousness, it is Love.

When a person is locked into their conditioned self, two things can happen with sex, it is either used to release negative personal insecurity issues or for providing the ego with a sense of power and domination over the other. For example common place issues like relief of past hurt and inner pain, personal insecurity and anger.

This is the case for both male and female but the behaviour is very different in the way is it lived out.

Another point of consideration in a male and some females is that when survival is threatened lust tends to manifest. For example a man who has just lost his job can experience overwhelming lustful thoughts and desires. This is nature raising the sexual energy to recreate itself, as the body feels threatened therefore may die. The need to reproduce the species comes into play. In today's society however we do not die with this type of thread but the primal instinct still exists and behaves accordingly.

The solution to these issues is the inner emotional security being rooted in love.

Love
Opening the Heart

- To support another is more important than telling them what to do

- You already know Love, for you are that Love at the centre of your heart

- The more you surrender to that inside of you the more your heart will flower in universal unconditional love

- Love only knows love therefore love attracts love

- To experience love from others you must first discover love inside yourself

- You are Love, therefore You are precious - Experience this and you will fully experience freedom from all emotional suffering!

- To fully awaken to Love, to fully experience Love you have to learn 'Acceptance of everything as it is, or has been'

- Acceptance comes when you 'stop judging others or yourself'

- Catch and stop your mind talking bad about others, stop gossiping and spreading rumours about others, accepting them as they are

- Allow others to be what they are

The Divine Message About You

- Start by being grateful for everything in your life, no matter how painful your experiences may have been

- Live in the present moment as this creates freedom from past suffering. This is because the event that caused the suffering is not happening now

- Surrender to the 'Love inside of you' that only exists in the now and ask the inner pure love to give you the experience of its unchanging Unconditional Love

- Love does not possess

- Love does not Judge

- Love only attracts Love

- If you want Love, become Love

- Within the energy of Love radiates the energy of Healing

- When the Heart opens, your inner knowingness or intuition of the great universal wisdom mind, 'Pure Awareness Mind' will arise in the present moment and guide your life on it's unique path

Uniqueness

A distressed women goes to see a marriage guidance councillor. To try and reconcile and re-create loving intimacy the therapist suggests "Why don't you go on a vacation?"

The woman being annoyed at the suggestion states "My husband does not go on vacations!"

The truth of this situation is that the therapist acting on knowingness from her own position or training she had received about relationship counselling, offers general advice that is supposed to be the solution to make a couple happy and rekindle their relationship.

The truth is that this does not help whatsoever and has the opposite effect by getting the client wild and feeling misunderstood.

Because all living beings are unique no one can offer advice to another. You can listen and ask questions to discover what the other already knows about themselves. In truth the wife has no understanding about her husband because we are uniquely different, although she might have invested a lot of time in trying to know him.

Key Points

All human beings are unique therefore no one can offer advice to another

The only commonness between human beings is the inner love and the source of light which created our life, pure awareness

All solutions to problems come from reconnection to universal love, once this is again felt no matter how the other is, all is right with the world

If the person is not connected to their own inner source of love they will compound the suffering of not being able to be understood by their significant other

The solution is Gentle Touch for Pure Love and Pure Awareness True-Self awakening.

This is the root problem for all relationships. The only solution is love and awareness. The amazing thing is this universe is full of love. It is very close and very personal. Once you are open to your inner love, then uniqueness becomes beautiful, not something to be understood but something which you share with others in a beautiful way, because we all become very, very special. There is no one exactly like you, this uniqueness then becomes your gift to mankind.

Please be mindful that you do not do what so many do and beat themselves up because they want to be like someone else. This is impossible. The answer is in nature. Go into a flower garden and look at a flower. Does the rose try and be anything else? Is one flower more beautiful than another? Ask people and everyone will have a different choice as to what they prefer. This is beautiful. One thing is for certain you will never see a flower in therapy!

The Love which you are seeking is seeking you - Right Now

Please remember this, so many seekers of God, of divinity, of pureness frantically enter the spiritual journey to escape the loneliness felt within the personality, denying their uniqueness because of the suffering they are feeling, because of the loneliness they experience. In truth once your connection to universal love and pure awareness of true self is established, your understanding and perception will change completely. At this point in your life you will get out the champagne, scream "Hooray" knowing that you have escaped from the limited separated self.

Just imagine the other side of this, if only the pure self was felt and experienced how boring existence would be then; just sameness, no contrast! I know that when I first had my awakening experience being bathed in eternal love, my mind was still asking questions about the beyond until a point of stillness arose and the questioner disappeared, being replaced by total contentment. After that a Golden perfection of everything in my daily life, in this world, was experienced. I am unable to tell you about life after death because to me there is no such thing because I am always eternally existing, right here, right now. The only change I experience today is in my body which is what creates the beauty of all this life experience.

Therefore the answer lies in awakening to love, awakening to your pure awareness self and living life uniquely for a lifetime. Yes, the truth is you need both because you are both. One without the other is emptiness without juice. I cannot tell you about your experience because you are unique. We are so privileged to have this short life containing everything of purity in our unchanging self connected to our uniqueness self, flowering into life in perfection.

In truth there is no separation between anything. Once the controller leaves the body/mind you flower in the radiance of the divine naturally. There is nothing to obtain, there is nothing to achieve, there is nothing to do. Once you become one or should I say you reconnect with the love that is seeking you, everything happens by itself and you just become 'the seeing' of the ever changing paradise of the moment to moment perfection.

What an amazing life we have! Let go and wake up to love and then everything will happen automatically, perfectly for your uniqueness.

Oneness Blessings of Love

Follow Your Heart
Inner Awareness and Inner Love

- It is natural for others to tell you what they want you to do

- Listen to others' points of view and respect their view

- Only act on your inner awareness and not what others are telling you

- You will know when it is right for you as you will get a nice feeling somewhere in your body, normally in your Heart

- Inside your body-mind-soul there is Pure Awareness which will guide you in your daily life

- You are perfect as you are

- Connect with this inner pure awareness

- Happiness and Love come from pure Awareness

- Pure Awareness does not think of what to do, it just knows the perfect thing to do in every moment of your life

- Love and Happiness exist within you, right now and never leave you

- This is known as inner heartfelt feeling or inner listening without thinking

The Divine Message About You

- 'Pure Awareness' replaces thinking - it is experienced more in the head area

- 'Pure Love' comforts and transforms all emotions and is felt in the heart or throughout the body

- "The sacred flame in my heart burns eternally, it never goes out so I am forever warm in the hands of my Beloved". *Robert Bourne*

The Awakening Process
Gentle Touch Practice Guide

We are constantly in an ever changing process of evolution with all of existence. It is important to understand that you are enlightened now, however the two pure oneness bodies of 'Eternal Love' and 'Pure Awareness' are not normally fully shining in your life. You do however connect with them at times without realising that it has happened, but for most of the time they are laying dormant, just waiting for you to put your attention upon them; this is what the practice of 'Gentle Touch' will do.

This means most people are blocking off two parts of themselves from being experienced. Therefore an adjustment to what you believe about yourself is initially required. In truth you are perfect now because you are these two bodies plus your own unique human body; the three create your True-Self-Being. These two pure bodies are regarded as oneness bodies because they are the same within everyone.

> The First belief to embrace - The two pure oneness bodies create an equality within the society of the world. They exist equally in everyone alongside the differences that each human being uniquely expresses.
>
> The Second belief to embrace is that you are connected to the two unchanging pure bodies. It is your body which they are trying to manifest through to enable you to have your unique divine human-being existence.

The Gentle Touch Practice

The first body of pure unchanging oneness consciousness is the body of Pure Awareness. This is male in nature and as such its light shines out throughout the whole of existence and is the light of pure awareness. It is this light which creates all of life, as it shines it creates form. As it slows down it changes into a type of waving omni-present form which becomes the second body of Love. As this light comes into the duality of life it creates all life forms. Through your Gentle Touch practice the Pure-Awareness-Self will reconnect you to this inner light bringing inner contentment and stillness of mind. The eventual realisation is that you and God are one; this is the Enlightenment of all spiritual masters. The key to this state is stillness of mind.

The second body of unchanging eternal love is connected to your heart through your emotional body. It is this energy which is very gently waving in form and is reflected inward, being feminine in nature. When resting in your Pure-Awareness-Self divine love presence becomes your natural aura. This is the Gentle Touch energy practice to reconnect you back to the Universal emotional body of love; the Spiritual Mother.

It is these two pure bodies you are going to reconnect with and open through your practice of Gentle Touch.

Pure Awareness - Divine Light
The First Pure Spiritual Body

The Light of Pure Awareness comes from the formless unchanging aspect of all of existence described as God, the Universal field, Void or whatever name you give it.

Deep within you, at your very core, the centre of your uniqueness is in total stillness. In your third eye you may see the light that never goes out, the eternal flame within all of life. In fact it is life before Love. It shines from nothingness outwards, hence it is the creator of all that is. It is untouchable hence it is eternally constant. It is this which created you, me and everything. This comes down from your crown chakra.

When you lose your attachments created by your limited mind as the controller of your life it is exchanged for your natural mind of pure awareness and everything flows in perfect harmony. Your life is then just put before you and this happens automatically. This mind is known as the awakened mind, being awakened and then living in the presence of love life just becomes a very beautiful experience.

Preparation for Awakening Pure Awareness
Know Nothing

- Drop all of what and who you think you are
- Drop all your beliefs and concepts about life

Doing this allows the alignment to reoccur with your Pure Awareness Self. When a connection is made to Pure Awareness this stimulates your true energy emotional body of Love to be experienced. This unchanging pure body is common to all living beings. This is why when experienced we never feel alone in a natural quality of meditation, inner peace and contentment. In stillness of pure awareness our natural aura is a Love Presence. Our body from the base chakra to the third eye is then filled with love which overflows into society which is why we can have love for everyone.

You become the creator without needing to desire anything because everything you need is put before you effortlessly. It is at this point of stillness that the thinking mind stops and the questioner disappears. In its place arises the contentment of not knowing, however when required in the moment, the wisdom of the external now arises to guide your choice making moment to moment life experiences.

If you are to live in freedom and express the beautiful unique human being that you are, you have to place your attention upon that which is at your very core right now. It is not hidden because it is your pure awareness, eternally existing. This Gentle Touch pure awareness practice will simply re-connect you to this eternal light to re-awaken a stillness unmoving mind of pure contentment and unshakable happiness.

Om Namo Bhagavate Vasudevaya
Mantra for Liberation connecting to Pure Awareness

Salutations to the Indweller who is omnipresent, omnipotent, immortal and Divine.

Mantra for liberation from the lower survival self as it calls upon the higher self to reside in the third eye, producing Pure Awareness, Divine universal wisdom. This mantra is called the Great Liberation Twelve-Syllable Mantra. It frees our minds and souls from negative patterns.

Om: Connection to source Divine manifestation

Namo: Salutations to *(the lower-self surrenders to embrace the inner divine-self)*

Bhagavate: This is referring to the body of Pure Awareness *(See the Moola Mantra about Bhagavate)*

Vasudevaya: Is the individual aspect of divinity that dwells inside of us. The energy that incarnates as an Avatar, the inner Guru God Self to help and guide us. This is our higher wisdom body self.

Om Namo: I bow to the subtle Divine inner wisdom.

The mantra starts with Om Namo so it is important to share what this means. This part of the mantra is saying that you surrender your ego in an attitude of graceful humility. You accept that your personal mind has to be surrendered, to be dropped to allow the light of pure awareness, of the Divine Truth to illuminate your limited mind. You can now see the connection and importance of 'Om Namo'.

Creating the Best Outcome

Remember that you are already enlightened; love everything without attachment or judgement, know nothing with certainty, make an inner space for your Divinity to manifest inside of you; allow your higher self to reside within your third eye to guide your life, whilst your mind rests in your true-self.

The more you can accept that you 'know nothing' in relation to the highest Divine consciousness the greater and quicker the transformation will occur.

Regular and consistent practice of this mantra gives us complete spiritual freedom: it frees us from the cycle of rebirth by releasing the mind from its attachments and helps us realise ourselves as a manifestation of transcendent Divinity.

Unconditional Love Presence
The Second Pure Spiritual Body

Divine Love Presence arises from Pure Awareness

The Gentle Touch practice connects to the highest source of eternal love. The practice opens the energy connection through the divine oneness crown chakra and awakens the heart chakra in the body. The pure energy will not be felt at the highest level but after you have chanted the Moola Mantra it will manifest as a natural aura.

The energy soon travels directly to the heart chakra causing it open, radiating pure love for all that is. Over time this causes a beautiful flowering of the heart to occur quite naturally without the need of any mind interference whatsoever.

When awakening happens your Divine-True-Self takes over your life. This means your mind will be resting in the centre of your pure-awareness being and the aura of divine love will surround you. Who would not want to live in causeless joy, bliss, peace, happiness and contentment with all your needs put before you without effort?

What has happened up to now is that your mind, thinking it is a separate person has been using the reflection of the divine light to create attachments with others based upon personal survival needs and personal desires; these desires are normally based upon the judgement of others.

Through awakening divine love presence all your connections and attachments will be transformed into divine consciousness. The body of love will then be the first connection to all others in this world.

Your mind/soul is now being transformed into the light of pure awareness. Your mind is going home to merge with your True-self allowing the divine to flow through your being without being controlled or limited by the minds attachments, especially those which are negatively binding to you.

Life's purpose is to live in endless eternal love, in the stillness of Pure Awareness. This is the Oneness of existence being expressed through its individual unique different life forms. We are all this.

Once experienced you can enjoy all other human beings, animals, the natural world and all of creation becomes an awesome wonder. It becomes a grateful privilege to be a human being. It becomes an eternal joy to be alive, right here, right now.

Awakening Divine Love Presence

The Moola Mantra represents a statement of the highest truth of all existence. The Moola Mantra explains in stages how the one-being becomes the many. It explains the spiritual workings of the whole of existence.

The Gentle Touch Practice awakens the two divine bodies; Sri Bhagavati which is the body of Pure Love together with Sri Bhagavate which is the body of Pure Awareness.

The Moola Mantra

Om Sat-Chit-Ananda, Para-Brahma
Purushothama, Paramatma
Sri Bhagavati Sametha, Sri Bhagavate Namaha

OM:	*inviting the higher divine energy*
SAT:	Divine Truth or Absolute Being
CHIT:	Pure Consciousness *infinite*
ANANDA:	Bliss
PARABRAHMA:	The Supreme Creator
PURUSHOTHAMA:	The energy that incarnates as an Avatar to help and guide mankind
PARAMATMA:	Supreme inner Divine consciousness in every living being; our pure all knowing higher self
SRI BHAGAVATI:	The female aspect, which is characterised as the supreme intelligence in the action of transformation; the power of pure love presence
SAMETHA:	*together with, in communion with*
SRI BHAGAVATE:	The male aspect of creation, which is unchangeable and permanent, this is the Pure Light Awareness - Truth
NAMAHA:	Saltations, I surrender my egoic mind to welcome and greet my inner divine-self. To join in union with our two pure bodies of Unconditional Love and Pure Awareness
HARI OM TAT SAT	Om, The Divine Absolute Truth

The Moola Mantra
Various Interpretations

Because this mantra is the core practice to achieve liberation and Awakening through the Gentle Touch practice, I was guided to provide as many interpretations as possible so you can obtain the understanding which best resonates with you.

My oneness friends all over the world have taken the trouble to share this with us through their websites. I have not made any amendments to their postings apart from anything which I have seen as discriminatory in nature; for example referring to the Divine as masculine.

This mantra evokes the living Infinite Being, asking protection and freedom from all sorrow and suffering. It is a prayer that adores the great creator and liberator, who out of love and compassion manifests, to protect us, in an earthly form. This Moola mantra has given great peace and joy to people all over the world, who have chanted, or even listened to it.

It has the power to transport ones mind to the state of causeless love and limitless joy. The calmness that the mantra can give is to be experienced, not spoken about. This mantra contains the key with which any door to spiritual treasure will be opened. A tool which can be used to achieve all desires. A medicine which cures all ills. The nectar that can set man free! All auspiciousness and serenity is yours simply by chanting or listening to this magnificent Moola mantra.

Whenever you chant this Vedic Sanskrit Mantra, even without knowing the meaning of it, that itself carries power. But when you know the meaning and chant it with feeling in your heart, then the energy will flow a million times more powerfully. It is therefore important to know the meaning of the Moola Mantra when you use it.

This Mantra is like calling a name. Just like when you call a person he comes and makes you feel his presence, in the same manner when you chant this mantra the Supreme Energy manifests everywhere around you. As the Universe is omnipresent, this Supreme Energy can manifest anywhere and anytime.

It is also very important to know that having a certain attitude of mind and emotions when chanting the Moola Mantra is important to activate the best connection with your inner Divine. This approach is in having deep humility, respect and a strong emotional desire as this will create a more open body mind, making the Divine Presence stronger.

Interpretation: Oh Divine Force, Spirit of All Creation, Highest Personality, Divine Presence, manifest in every living being, Supreme Soul manifested as the Divine Mother and as the Divine Father, I bow in deepest reverence.

The Moola Mantra Meaning

Om

It is the primordial sound or the Universal sound by which the whole universe vibrates. Om also means inviting the higher divine core being energy.

Sat Chit Ananda

The beginning of the mantra is 'Sat Chit Ananda Para-Brahma' which refers to the infinite being's state of consciousness. This state is eternal and unchanging. All those who have awakened to this state of being experience the same quality of ultimate enlightened Truth, pure consciousness at the highest enlightened state with the emotional experience of Bliss and unshakable happiness, no matter what is happening in the consciousness realms of constant change. This is the pure centre of our being and the core of all existence.

Sat - Truth or Absolute Being. Sat describes an essence that is pure and timeless, that never changes. The all penetrating existence that is formless, shapeless, omnipresent, attribute less, and quality less aspect of the Universe. It is the Un-manifest. It is experienced as the emptiness of the Universe. We could say it is the body of the Universe that is static. Everything that has a form and that can be sensed, evolved out of this Un-manifest. It is so subtle that it is beyond all perceptions. It can only be seen when it has become manifest into existence and has taken form. We are in the Universe and the Universe is in us. We are the effect and Universe is the cause and the cause manifests itself as the effect.

Chit

The Pure Consciousness of the Universe that is infinite, omni-present manifesting power of the Universe. Out of this is evolved everything that we call Dynamic energy or force. It can manifest in any form or shape. It is the consciousness manifesting as motion, as gravitation, as magnetism, etc. It is also manifesting as the actions of the body, as thought force. It is the Supreme Spirit.

Ananda

Bliss, unshakable happiness, love and friendship nature of the Universe. When you experience either the Supreme Energy in this Creation (Sat) and become one with the Existence or experience the aspect of Pure Consciousness (Chit), you enter into a state of Divine Bliss and eternal happiness (Ananda). This is the primordial characteristic of the Universe, which is the greatest and most profound state of ecstasy that you can ever experience when you relate with your higher Consciousness.

Parabrahma

The Supreme Being in its Absolute aspect; one who is beyond space and time. It is the essence of the Universe that is with form and without form. It is the Supreme creator.

Purushothama

This has different meanings. Purusha means soul and Uthama means the supreme, the Supreme spirit. It also means the supreme energy of force guiding us from the highest world. Purusha also means Man, and Purushothama is the energy that incarnates as an Avatar to help and guide Mankind and relate closely to the beloved Creation.

Paramatma

The supreme inner energy that is immanent in every creature and in all beings, living and non-living. It's the indweller, the inner Sat Guru or the Antaryamin who resides formless or in any form desired. It is the force that can come to you whenever you want and wherever you want to guide and help you.

Sri Bhagavati

The female aspect, which is characterised as the Supreme Intelligence in action, the Power (The Shakti). It is referred to the Mother Earth (Divine Mother) aspect of the creation.

Sametha

Together or in communion with

Sri Bhagavate

The Male aspect of the Creation, which is unchangeable and permanent.

Namaha

Salutations or prostrations to the Universe that is Om and also has the qualities of Sat Chit Ananda, that is omnipresent, unchangeable and changeable at the same time, the supreme spirit in a human form and formless, the indweller that can guide and help in the feminine and masculine forms with the supreme intelligence. I seek your presence and guidance all the time.

Om Tat Sat Definition

Om Tat Sat is a mantra in Sanskrit that is translated to mean the 'Supreme Absolute Truth' Literally 'All that is'. This Sanskrit mantra is translated to mean the 'Supreme Absolute Truth' everything in creation 'All that is'.

Om refers to the Supreme Infinite Spirit or Person.

Tat refers to 'that', or 'all that is'.

Sat refers to 'truth', that which is eternal constant, never changing as opposed to the aspect of life which is in constant change. This is the underlying basis to existence which is most fundamental and universal.

Hari Om Definition

This is sometimes chanted is Hari Om Tat Sat (Hari, the Lord, is infinite spirit - that is the truth) is also spoken as a variation, especially amongst followers of the Bhakti paths.

Hari Om: 'Hari' is another name for the Divine which can only mediate upon itself 'Om'. Therefore Om can follow Hari as Om usually comes first in a mantra.

Two words that are part of most mantras

OM This sound is usually chanted at the beginning of every mantra. It is known as a 'seed sound'. A seed sound is extremely potent and expresses a particular energy. A translation will always fall short and is actually impossible. Om is the sound of the sixth chakra, also known as The Third Eye. Here is where the masculine and feminine energies meet. It is called the Soundless Sound, or the Sound of the Universal (God/Divine) essence.

The King of mantras of a single syllable is 'Om'. It is the sound of infinity and immortality, containing within it all the scriptures of the world. 'Om' is often used at the beginning of meditation to focus the mind, or as a prefix to other mantras.

NAMAHA: A common ending to many mantras, means 'I offer my self'

NAM or NAMO: Used at the beginning of a mantra to state I embrace my life, to open and reveal the highest Divine nature. Namo means 'I bow' (to surrender the ego) taken from Namaste – 'The Divine in me greets the Divine in you'.

The Gentle Touch Practice
The Pure Awareness Body of Light Preparation

The 'Pure Awareness Body of Light' connection starts by accepting that whatever you think you know and believe in can become your barrier to the ultimate Truth. This is why centring yourself in the present moment is the starting point to dropping the thinking mind. A surrender is required by accepting a state of mind, that of not knowing, the enlightened mind of pure awareness self can then manifest.

Preparation of Intention - You pre-set one goal. Know what you are wanting to manifest before you start. Your desire is to have anything you wish to manifest for yourself; materially, physically or spiritually.

You now surrender your ego, your limited thinking mind to your inner God-Self.(*dropping all beliefs and any form of spiritual practice, visualisation or meditation techniques you have previously learnt*). You enter into a passive, humble, receiving mode of not knowing.

The Gentle Touch Mantras

To activate in the process of awakening you need to take action. To allow the effects of your action to take place you need to stay silent resting the mind and doing nothing at all.

You will see this pattern happening as you take part in the Gentle Touch Practice. First you chant a mantra and then you stay in silence; this is being active and then passive.

You now start the CD and let it play

1. Chant with Om Namo Bhagavate Vasudevaya
2. Stay in silence and listen to the ashram version track Listening Bhagavate
3. Chant with loving emotion The Moola Mantra
4. Stay in silence whilst listening to the Divine Presence Integration

It is AFTER you have chanted the Moola Mantra and you have entered into silence that the Divine Love Presence can be felt or sensed.

The creation of your goal is now taking place. No thinking or trying is required, the highest state of creation will do this for you from out of the mystical silence. Any negative aspects of the conditioned self are switched off when resting in this pure awareness state of consciousness.

Just allow your inner Divine-True-self to do what it has to do to transform your life. Just rest your mind in its love and start living from Being, not doing!

The Function of the Gentle Touch Mantras

Track 01 - Om Namo Bhagavate Vasudevaya

The purpose of chanting this track is to detached from and slow down the chattering mind to connect with the stillness of your Pure-Awareness-Self.

Track 02 - Ashram Om Namo Bhagavate Vasudevaya

Stay in silence with this track. The purpose of this track is to rest in the natural inner silence of your Pure-Awareness-Self.

Track 03 - Moola Mantra

This is the key track to chant or sing along with using passionate loving emotion. This mantra will align you to Universal Unconditional Oneness Love body through the divine crown chakra.

Track 04 - Love Presence Integration

Stay in silence with this track. This track allows the for a direct Love Presence connection to be anchored into the body to allow transformation to take place. Pay attention to the energy presence around your body. Stay in stillness of mind.

This energy could flow between your hands through the chakra system but you may not experience it in this way it all depends upon the individual both are okay. The presence is more of a natural loving aura surrounding all of your body. This presence arises naturally because you are resting in the stillness of your True-Self. It is like the fragrance of the divine itself manifesting to interact with all in your daily life with the presence of love.

This track was created for energy integration as it allows time for you to integrate the pure invisible Sat-Chit-Ananda energy experience by staying in silence. You may want or need to lay or sit down and just stay in silence to integrate the Divine energy.

Because everyone will experience this uniquely you will have to go with how you are being moved. There is no wrong way to experience this.

For maximum benefit a daily practice is recommended

Gentle Touch Group Practice

It is certainly a benefit to synchronise your Gentle Touch Practice with like minded others. If you are unable to meet together in the same room as a group then you can arrange a date and time to practice which will start all at the same time. I have found the benefit of practicing in a group together or by long distance is that the transformation power is increased and awakening is more easily achieved.

I have suggested that after downloading the New Awakening Process you start a community or support group. The Gentle Touch Practice is recommended to be one of the practices you come together within a group once a week.

After a Group Practice
Should we share our Experience?

Please remember if you are in a group that wants to share experiences everybody is unique, therefore you cannot compare your experience with another in terms of how you are doing. What you are experiencing is always perfect because you are unique.

Some people only notice the real effect a day or a few days afterwards, therefore sharing should be spontaneous and certainly not a ritual. This practice is coming from the unfelt, unseen, un-manifest Core Being, therefore it is beyond the five senses and its effects are mystical in nature.

When we have shared in the past what I have noticed which is interesting is that there will be some common phenomena happening although there can be many differences.

For sharing please split into small groups of four otherwise if the group becomes too large then there will not be enough time listen to everyone who wants to share.

The other point is that some people need to integrate the energy through lying down in silence and not want to share. After the energy is activated, the body tends to become very relaxed, as if in sleep. When this occurs it is a good idea to keep yourself warm. A blanket is good for this so you may need to take one to your group. If you are in your own home on your own have one ready to use one in case you need it.

The key is to be flexible and just go with how you are feeling at the final stage of the oneness love integration of the body/mind stage of the Gentle Touch practice.

Enjoy and Blessings of Love

Life After Awakening - Transformation

The reason why most people are out of touch with their natural emotional centre of the love body of their True-self is because today's society requires our attention to be focused on the outside. Because of society demands, people's minds are moving too quickly, consumed with constantly thinking about the future or the past through the use of mobile phones, social media networks, work, etc. Not being in the present moment is causing them to block off their emotional body, moving them away from the universal love heart energy to become stuck in the thinking judgmental mind.

Life after awakening? This is where so many spiritual seekers who are at the third stage of evolution have so much trouble.

It goes like this, "I have experienced bliss, causeless joy or have experienced the sense of freedom from the mind but unpleasant things are still happening, or the mind is still chattering so I maybe have not made it?"

The problem is that the early stage of awakening is delicate and it is very easy to be pulled back into past unwanted behavioural patterns or other people's traumas and life's expectancies, beliefs and experiences. The mind is still in existence with its illusionary attachments and it is this which needs to be transformed through daily life.

Now a person has learnt for many lifetimes that they have to be the 'doer' because they are all alone in this world. How can this habit be broken when you are told that when you are in your perfect centre of your awareness-self and you are now witnessing life from this place of True Self?

At the time when awakening first occurs through your regular practice of Gentle Touch, when you become de-clutched from the thinking mind, real transformation of the mind begins.

You need to stay alert so you don't react in a defensive protective personal way. As soon as you recognise the situation is uncomfortable you surrender your response to allow the presence of divine love to meet what is happening and transform the situation. This will also start your real transformation of the minds attachments.

Life at this stage of awakening now gets met by your inner God-Self which is pure love and pure awareness.

Let me repeat what you do one more time. When you meet an unpleasant life experience you immediately rest the mind, don't react in your normal automatic personhood state of mind. You now pass the experience to the presence of love which will transform the situation. Doing nothing becomes everything happening!

If you identify with the present moment as yours, or your entangled life experience with others, (known as mind attachments) you will normally get caught into the pattern of your previous response and re-create it again.

The key to change therefore is to stay detached and become a witness to what is happening. When you do this, provided you are in your pure awareness self, the Divine presence will greet the moment and transform it into Divine consciousness.

Staying with the present moment, resting in your true self, will allow the presence of Divine love to transform you completely. Over time the mind/soul will unfold until it completely dissolves all attachments and comes to rest as a pure enlightened being. This is the state of all enlightened masters.

Patience, acceptance of what is manifesting in your life without judgement and most importantly trust are the keys to establishing faith in your True-God-Self. Until such times as a stability occurs and there is no-thinking-mind, an acceptance of everything as it is in its perfect Divine flowering of various states of consciousness is required, without judgement.

A daily practice of Gentle Touch is the solution to a rapid transformation. In the download for the 'New Awakening Process' two supporting help guides are now available.

Two Supporting Help Guides

- Sri Ramana Maharshi Self-enquiry Teachings
- Awakening Guidance by Sri Bhagavan

You will find that reading the Sri Ramana Maharshi teachings, enclosed in the website download, will explain in detail about the attachments of the mind.

Sri Bhagavan from the oneness university in India has a comprehensive commonly asked questions with answers about the Awakening Process. I have included conversations with awakened human beings who have transformed their lives and are now living in a no-person existence.

Creating a CD for Your Gentle Touch Practice Technical Help using iTunes

You could create a CD for your practice using iTunes. You will need to create a new playlist in the order listed above. The following pathway in iTunes is how you create playlist: File - New - Playlist. You then need to add the four tracks to the playlist, as in the Gentle Touch Practice Mp3s provided.

01 Om Namo Bhagavate

02 Listening Bhagavate

03 Moola Mantra

04 Divine Presence Integration

Once you have created a playlist you can create a CD select the following pathway and settings: File - Burn playlist to disc - Disc format = Audio CD (Use a CD-R 700MB 80 min disc is fine)

The difference between Audio CD format and Mp3

By selecting Audio CD format it will play in any CD player. The older units do not play Mp3 files. If all your players including your car are modern they will all play Mp3 files.

The difference between a CD and Mp3 disc is that you can only get about 12 songs or 80 mins playing time in the conventional CD format, whereas a Mp3 disc will play about 120 songs on the same disc!

So for the Gentle Touch Practice both formats will fit onto a standard CD disc.

About the Author
How the Sacred Teachings Emerged

I wondered why I was selected to receive these sacred teachings. This chapter provides a background about my life experiences which culminated in me having this experience.

Ever since this knowledge was downloaded into my mind at the end of 2014 I have been aware that a sort of completion has happened to my life in terms that this has been the purpose of my incarnation. I know that I have nothing else to do except to share these teachings with the whole world. My role is now nothing else but one of attuning others to their own inner divinity. I am here in the role of helping support others who also wish to experience this beautiful state of existence.

In the book it talks about the three stages of a person's evolution and transformation of the soul body. It is this which I will share with you in context about my own life's experiences.

The First Stage of Robert's Evolution

This first stage of our life's existence we all know and experience. It is living life as a separate person with a physical body containing an inner emotional and mental self awareness; the person tends to be guided by religion or just relies upon their own mind. At this stage we have free will which is limited to within our conditioned personality.

Within eighteen months of my birth I was adopted by a working class family, providing me the privilege of being brought up in a small village in the delightful West Sussex countryside. One of the conditions of my adoption was that I was brought up with the Church of England religion. My Mother was an old fashioned 'upstairs downstairs' cook working in service to the gentry; as such she was obedient to the letter. As a result I became an Altar boy, became part of the choir, attended Bible classes and was receiving Holy Communion.

As a small boy I remember having conversations with the local Vicar about God and when he could not supply a suitable answer I would inform him that he did not know what he was talking about and what he had said was not true. I then lost respect for him in terms of my source of spiritual guidance and became disillusioned with what the Church could offer me.

Thereafter the highlight of the church service always used to be watching the snuff-taking organ player leave when the Vicar was starting his sermon and returning just in time before he finished talking. It was only years later that I discovered he had gone go the local village pub, the Anchor, to consume a quick pint and rush back in time to play the organ after the sermon had finished.

I had no awareness of my spiritual nature but in my late teens was fascinated with creating an Altar, lighting candles and burning incense, much to my adopted family's realisation that I was unusual, not fitting into the family life activities very well.

I left home around the age of seventeen after my parents separated, having dutifully stayed together purely for the sake of the children. My upbringing was within a loveless marriage.

This lack of emotional love experience caused me to fall in love with the first girlfriend I met and eventually marry just one year later. We moved to Manchester, had two children and lived an emotionally unstable relationship; we were both damaged emotionally from our previous lives' experiences. Needless to say we soon parted, eventually to become divorced.

During this time between the ages of 20 to 30 I worked very hard to make something of my life, ending up with several businesses, achieving all the material trimmings of owning a couple of properties and a fancy car with enough money not to have to work.

Everything was roses apart from my love-life! In my mid twenties I remarried, but within a few years my second wife left me for another man. My material life was fine but my emotional life was a nightmare. During these ten years I was a musician and a business man until one day my limited company went into liquidation and overnight I lost everything.

At this time I had gained a good reputation in the Manchester area for running several successful businesses and was invited to become a director of a friend's company. It was at this point I decided, "Enough, no more business. I need time out."

Looking back on this time I can relate this to astrology and can see that I had the classic Saturn return, wherein a person is able to look back and review their life's experiences.

I then asked the question about how society had conditioned me. If I have achieved all the things we are told to do, get a good job or become successful by running your own business, make loads of money, get married have a family, take a good pension and live happily ever after, why wasn't I happy?

The happily ever after did not happen for me as I had achieved all of this dream by the age of thirty, only to lose everything society tells you to do to be fulfilled and happy.

As this was not true for me I blamed myself and thought there was something in me that must be causing all the problems in my life. I realised that I needed to change this program on the inside. Alongside this realisation I also went into the mode of asking many profound seeking questions like "What is this world all about?" "Why are we here?" "What is this life really about as there must be something more than what we are told to become?"

The Second Stage of Robert's Evolution

Having asked the question, "What is the meaning of life?" I never realised I had set in motion the inner spiritual aspect of my being to start guiding me. I was set on a path towards spiritual awakening. The person Robert had now become a spiritual seeker.

The Second Stage of evolution happens when the person realises that they are not separate from others in the world and become responsible for their own experiences, instead of blaming others for what happens to them. The person then enters upon a spiritual seeking journey to discover their higher or inner spiritual self; the person tends to choose their spiritual teachers instead of the religion they were born into.

At this time I was living with my girlfriend who was a professional singer. I decided to form a band around her as her lead guitarist. This was the first time in my life I became a full-time musician.

After being on the road with the band for a couple of years the band won a resident contract at a Swiss ski resort leaving my girlfriend and myself to continue performing on our own as a duo. Before the band disbanded we went into the studio and recorded backing tapes of our stage act.

The duo went on to become a main supporting act to big stars at private functions. It was at one of these functions we were working with a famous Hypnotic act. I was fascinated by this phenomena and that evening chatted with the Hypnotist backstage to discover that he taught hypnotherapy professionally at a famous Harley Street Clinic. I undertook his training and qualified as Hypnotherapist in March of 1986.

I went on as many courses I could to gain mastery of my new profession. I also studied many complementary therapies. I had my first spiritual awakening experience in Scarborough when attending a week's intensive master hypnotist training course. The course consisted solely of experiencing hypnotic inductions, where a small group of students spent a whole week going in and out of trance.

I remember that evening calling my girlfriend to share that I had changed emotionally and that we could resolve the relationship difficulties we were then experiencing. Unfortunately she was not interested in change, hence eventually leading to our separation.

After our parting I was living on my own within a large shared house in Manchester. One Sunday evening I was feeling sad about having separated from my girlfriend and was watching the television. A documentary about Krishnamurti was being shown and everything he was saying I was saying. Yes that's right, yes this man was describing the experience I had just had. At last someone else understood. He was the first person I heard describe the inner experience I had just had on my course. My sadness immediately vanished and I no longer felt alone. I felt that at last someone knew what I was talking about.

After that experience I was obsessed with spiritual awakening, specifically in healing and the helping of others. I went through some unusual experiences which I would like to share with you.

My first unusual connection started happening when a crow would come and sit in a tree outside my bedroom window and talk directly to me; he used to give me messages about what I had to do. I never questioned this and regarded that this was a message from spirit. I therefore followed whatever he had to say.

One of the abilities that had spontaneously awoken in me was that when I met someone I could instantly see all their past lives and their future lives to come. I now know this as transfiguration where the person's face changes rapidly showing all the different people they have been in previous lives. I did not do anything about this spiritual phenomena.

One day a crow arrived with another message informing me that I had to move to London. I somehow had a knowing that this was true but was reluctant to move. Eventually I did and made the appropriate arrangements to set off for London. I left what little personal possessions I had with a friend and set off on my new journey to discover what fate had planned for me in London.

When I arrived in London I went to the clinic in Harley Street to say hello to my hypnotherapy teacher, only to discover he was not there. The owner of the clinic took a shine to me and after a practical interview I was given the position as their consultant hypnotherapist and sports psychologist at her famous Harley Street clinic. Until I found somewhere to live I was allowed to stay in the clinic.

With this new work position I engaged a professional secretarial phone answering service so my clients could leave a message to a person and not a machine. One day I received a message from a lady living in St Johns Wood, London. After calling her back she said she had no knowledge of leaving me a message. The conversation went something like this "Hello it is Robert Bourne, consultant hypnotherapist. Thank you for your message, how can I help you?" "I have not left you a message. Are you calling about the flat we have to rent?" "No, but I am looking for somewhere to live".

We went on to share about our mutual spiritual interests where she revealed that she also was a spiritual healer. At this point we were still confused about how I received her message but were now much more interested in meeting each other.

I arrived at an impressive luxury block of flats, got into the lift, walked to the door and rang the doorbell. I was greeted by a beautiful lady with long dark hair. We were both speechless as we gazed at each other for a short while. I was then invited inside to a large reception area and was quickly told that she had been waiting for me to arrive for a long time.

She was a spiritual healer and ran a regular psychic development group. She informed me that at the group messages were coming about this man that was going to visit them. All they were told is that this person had previously been one of the Middle Eastern master's disciples. To prepare for the visit to come they had to provide a gift of a dishdasha gown for him to wear. *(The dishdasha is the traditional Arabian clothing for men.)*

We both entered into a deeply spiritual connection and our sharing went on for ages. It was apparent that there was much more to be discovered between us so I was invited to stay in the spare room. I did stay with her for about two weeks without leaving. I made arrangements with my friends and my work that I would not available for a time unknown.

It was that evening that she brought the gown to my room and was rather embarrassed to ask me if I would please put it on. She told me that two days earlier she was told by her spirit guides to shorten the gown as it was too long. Well, I happily obliged her as this experience was very exciting for me. The gown fitted me perfectly. This confirmed to her that I was the man that was prophesied to visit her.

That evening when we eventually got to bed the gown was hanging up on display so I put it on again and had a strange experience. I looked down at my feet to see them disappearing. Yes, it looked like a bodily dematerialisation, something only normally seen on 'beam be up Scottie' on Star Trek. Anyway I cannot say how long this dematerialisation happened for but I did come back again.

Events like this continued to happen. For example we were taken by spiritual guides to visit the old healing home of the famous healer Harry Edwards. Another time we were sitting in Regents Park watching the geese flying backwards!

Although this was fascinating our coming together had created something quite supernatural. I was still emotionally feeling unhappy as I had become infatuated with this girl, which was not returned. I soon left her company to continue my spiritual journey to find inner love and happiness.

It must have been around 1987 when I went to my first Buddhist meeting and started chanting Nam Myoho Renge Kyo. This chanting practice was taught by an organisation called NSUK, Nichiren Shoshu United Kingdom with the sole purpose of creating world peace through the change of the individual.

I devoted myself to this practice for many years and had realised that I had a past life connection with the priesthood and the first president of the SGI, Soka Gakkai International. As I chanted I felt like I was a priest and this is all I wanted to become in this life. I was also very interested in Education for Creative Living, a system of value creating education based upon direct life experience through creating valuable human beings. I had a strong desire to visit the head temple at Taisekiji in Japan based at Mount Fuji. I had no money for this venture but started chanting a million mantras to achieve this goal.

A Japanese foreign student visited one of my Buddhist group meetings and was so impressed with my faith and determination that she offered to host my visit to Japan. This lead to staying with her in Tokyo and visiting her family in Osaka. She made all the arrangements for my week long visit to be filled full of experience; typical Japanese organisation style.

It was November 1990 when I was greeted by Mariko at Tokyo airport where she took me back to her office which was at a merchant bank. She then sent me off in a taxi to her flat to wait for an SGI member to meet me and look after me until she had finished her work.

The Japanese lady arrived at midday bringing a variety of food for me to eat. Not speaking Japanese and she could not speak English I was taken to a large gathering of Japanese SGI Buddhists at their main Tokyo cultural centre. I was the only foreign person at this meeting. The centre was huge and after some time the meeting was about to start and we were taken to a large hall with a stage. I was ushered to the front to discover that the leader of the SGI had summoned all the senior leaders in Japan to a special meeting where he announced that the SGI lay members had separated from the priesthood as they had fallen out about various issues, thereby a schism had occurred.

After the meeting I said my goodbyes to everyone and set off on my own to another part of Tokyo where I was meeting one of the priests at his temple. Before my visit to Japan I had known about this arrangement to meet the priest and having had the skill of intuitive aromatherapy was spiritually guided to make a special blend of oils for the priest I was about to meet.

The priest and myself had a lovely meeting and exchanged gifts. I received a lovely set of sandalwood prayer beads and to his surprise I had a gift for him. It transpired that he had a chest infection which he was not able to clear; yes the oil was his medicine. He mentioned that I was like his brother and that I had been a priest in previous lifetimes as Buddhism was not new to me.

That evening he took me to a restaurant in the middle of Tokyo where my host Mariko rejoined us after she had finished her work. I could not believe what an eventful day I had had.

Later that week I visited the head temple, again I was the only Westerner to attend the ceremony. When I saw the original Gohonzon, an inscribed scroll that Buddhists use in their chanting practice, I had this overwhelming desire to stand up and remonstrate, as my inner knowingness knew this was not the original Gohonzon as it was reported to be.

After the experience the final part of my week was spent with Mariko's lovely family in Osaka. A school visit was arranged to see the Soka schools because of my known interest. A member of Mariko's family attended a junior Soka school which enabled the visit to happen. I was very fortunate being in the right place at the right time, as it was the end of term and all the heads of the schools system were present for the end of term closing ceremony. After this had taken place all the children went home and I was privileged to meet the heads of the school system and had a question and answer session about Education for Creative Living.

It was at this meeting I was invited by one of the teachers to visit a nearby senior high school in Osaka. My hosts were excited at doing this so we went and had a lovely tour of this very special school. Whilst I was there the head of English offered me a job with them for a three year contract teaching English. I willingly accepted and said I would get my teaching qualification on my return to England. This was an opportunity to learn about how the school system worked and bring the knowledge back to Europe with the view of opening new Value Creating Schools.

When I was back in England a year later in 1991 it was announced to the world the schism of the Buddhist organisation was official. The members at that time were asked to choose to practice with the priests or stay with the SGI. I could not choose either as I loved them all. I then took a step back not knowing what to do.

I studied my TEFL qualification (Teaching English as a foreign Language). I was living in Cheltenham at the time so I rented out my house to move to Bournemouth to gain some teaching experience in some language schools in 1992 before I set off to Japan.

I never went to Japan as the offer was withdrawn and I was left in Bournemouth but did not see myself as a TEFL teacher. I remember one evening looking out to sea as I stood on the pier wondering "What was that all about?". Hello here was that question arising again. Anyway I decided to go back to my music, formed a duo and enjoyed living in Bournemouth.

During this time I was disappointed with the Buddhist organisation as I felt that they had let me down. This caused me to look deeper and investigate what The Lotus Sutra was really about. If the Buddha said it is the cause for all enlightenment then I had not experienced it. I wanted to have the same experience Christ and Buddha had had. I then retreated to my flat, took down my Gohonzon, and studied two copies of the Lotus Sutra chanting for weeks over each chapter.

I was having mystical knowingness experiences of divine wisdom arise and could verify The Lotus Sutra contained the mystical truth of enlightenment.

I then spent my time in another spiritual practice of loving everything as if I was meeting God. I mustered what amount of love I had and embraced everything if I was in a deep love affair with the whole world. If anyone would have seen me I would definitely have been described as a madman. One day I was sitting contentedly sending out love. It was then returned a million fold and I had a kundalini awakening experience. I experienced an ocean of universal love which never stopped; it was an eternal omni-present source. I discovered that I could connect with this source at will, just like opening and closing the curtains of a window that were blocking out the light. The year I had this experience was 1995, some 20 years before writing this book.

The Third Stage of Robert's Evolution

The Third Stage of evolution happens when the person experiences that the divine and the unique human being are one; this is known as Mysticism. The conditioned person with its inherited genetic family tendencies of positive and negative is transformed and transcended into a state known as Awakening. In this state the person no longer exists and 'free will' is replaced with acceptance of the perfect ever-changing moment in a blissful, joyful, loving all-knowing state of life; this is awakening into the enlightenment of being-ness.

I certainly had experienced this state of being. In this state I only had one desire which was to help others also experience their own awakening. I got people together first of all to share the loving presence that emerged from within me whenever I opened the curtain to the light. This was verified as true by the experiences others automatically were having such as; spontaneous healing, connection to inner love and receiving divine answers to their seeking questions.

One evening I went out to a dance where I decided to let the love presence out for everyone to enjoy. A big mistake as it caused chaos. Some people started shaking whilst others were getting very angry. In the Gentle Touch practice guide I talk about this phenomena and why this can happen when divine love is experienced.

Anyway at the dance I stopped letting the presence out and left immediately. I was then very confused about how I was going to share this universal love. My inner divine master told me that I am not to let this out in public. I replied "Then I had better create an ashram with warning signs outside." I was told that, no you have done this before in a past life and there are others here playing this role; you are here to support them.

You can imagine I was confused. I had had a divine love awakening experience, fully experienced the Buddha's mystical divine wisdom Lotus Sutra but was unable to share it because it was too strong a connection for people to directly experience.

Just getting on with daily living it was in 2003 that I was informed that I was to learn and teach Reiki Healing. I was surprised because healing is a very gentle easily accessible energy that comes out of divine love. I accepted this direction and was informed that I was to provide a foundation of teachings to help people awaken. I was told that healing is a pure energy connection with the angelic realm and will start transforming a person to prepare them to experience unconditional love. This was to be a preparation for something else for mankind's evolution.

Today you can get a copy of all the three degrees of New Awakening Reiki Healing form my Naturally You website. I have created home study courses in full multimedia containing the Reiki manuals, audio tutorials and videos. There are also self attunement videos which you can use to attune yourself to the inner divine very easily.

Alongside these teachings a set of companion wisdom courses are available called 'The Seekers Guide for a New Awakening', which was published in 2009. I was informed that the introduction in this book was to present an overview of the Oneness phenomena being released in India by Sri Amma Bhagavan. The book also contains three courses to help with the three stages of evolution. The truths in the book will prepare a person for stage three of their spiritual journey, full awakening into divine presence.

In 2011 I met with sat guru Sri Mooji in satsang on a retreat course in London. When I arrived at the venue I was informed that I was to create a double album sacred mantra CD. I mentioned this to Mooji and asked him if I could dedicate the CD to him and record any of his favourite mantras. He agreed and said Sri Ram Jai Ram was one he enjoyed. In 2012 the album was released.

This CD has a transformational experience to achieve 'Freedom from the Conditioned Self'. For those who have obtained this awakened state of freedom from the conditioned self, a deepening of the enlightened state will occur until the final transformation of Buddahood when the Sat Guru awakening manifests.

Part One of the CD: Mantras 1-5 The journey begins with Sita Ram inviting God, the Divine into the heart. In mantras 2-5 a going home experience happens by moving down from the head to the heart chakra.

Part Two of the CD: Mantras 6-8 - The heart has now been prepared for the dissolving of soul illusions through embracing Shiva in mantras 6-7. The final step is to awaken the inner Sat Guru ~ Brahma Nandam ~ Mantra 8.

You can use this CD to hold your own sacred mantra singing group. To create an awakening experience the sacred mantras have been carefully selected from direct feedback of many Sacred Mantra circles I have held. The mantras only contain the original root Sanskrit words; all additional wording has been removed; in doing this the mind is not engaged in the experience, leaving an emptiness for the Divine to become reflected in the mind.

It was in 2013 a modern interpretation from my direct awakening experience of 'The Lotus Sutra' was publishing in a book entitled 'You are a Buddha not a Person'. For those wishing to experience this as a practice, an ancient Chinese melody has been used to create a Mantra which can be chanted when reading the book to awaken divine universal wisdom.

'You are a Buddha not a Person' is a modern easy to understand interpretation of the Buddha's mystical teaching of enlightenment 'The Lotus Sutra'. It was this Sutra which brought about my own enlightenment of the 'Buddhist Treasure Tower' experience which occurred over 20 years ago.

This book is written from the inner guru of Buddha Wisdom and will reveal how all spiritual teachings in the world have been created by the Divine (Buddha Nature) as a way to prepare and lead people to the Awakened state of 'No Person Existence'.

The book goes on to reveal how Sri Amma Bhagavan from the Oneness University in India are behaving like the Buddha in the Lotus Sutra and how the 'Oneness Deeksha Blessing' is a means for awakening the spiritual preparation inside mankind in this age. Yes, now is the time to Awaken to your True Self.

It was now 2015 and believed that everything had been created that was required to help others. I felt I had finished with this role as I was empty from past known phenomena and had done a good job in helping those who were interested in their own awakening process. It was then that Gentle Touch was born.

I wanted to share the experiences in my life because I can see looking back how everything has been perfect. I can see that from my enlightenment experience I was guided to prepare practices that fit together to support the awakening process contained within this book.

The Gentle Touch practice starts with the healing energy before a sacred mantra is chanted to quiet the mind to evoke the pure light of awareness to come forth. Chanting this mantra enables the karmic mind to transform and for you to experience a calmness and stillness of mind which is the universal oneness mind, common within us all.

From this state of being the Deeksha energy of unconditional love is invoked by chanting the Moola Mantra. I have now released a download version of the Moola Mantra by Robert Bourne which is available from all suppliers like iTunes, Amazon etc.

The Gentle Touch practice uses the method of bringing down a golden ball of energy from the divine crown chakra to the personal heart chakra in the body of the human being. Pure divinity and duality become one at this point. The Divine presence becomes anchored in the body.

The final aspect of the practice occurs when the love energy Golden Ball guides the individual around the room in a Tai Chi like movement. When the mantra is finished everybody in the room stands still and shares their golden ball of love energy with each other.

I could not have created this without over the last eight years first creating the parts which are required within the new practice of Gentle Touch.

The amazing thing is that everyone who practices Gentle Touch has it easy as the pathway has been created by myself, all the Oneness Deeksha givers, Sri Mooji and Sri Bhagavan.

Finally thank you for reading this book and if it has inspired you and you want to be part of a new world based upon love and care for each other then please join us at Gentle Touch. Don't worry you will not be conditioned any more by Gentle Touch because this about setting you free to blossom into the unique human being you are meant to be.

Robert Bourne

The Love and Awareness Awakening Process Creator
of
'Gentle Touch Awakening to Oneness Love'

- My role is to get you through, to help you awaken

- Because I have made it

- Because I have fully experienced Eternal Unconditional Love

- Because I am resting in Contentment

- Because happiness is always present

Autobiography

- I am here to help you, to reassure you

- Because you are perfect now

- Because I live in Abundance

- I wait 'in love' for you

- Because emotions come and go in the moment being cleansed by love

- Because knowingness arises in the moment within me

- I am here to guide you to fully experience all of what I have obtained

- I will tell you the truth because 'I love you'

- I will point you to the many great enlightened beings on the planet

- This awakening process is about 'all of us'

- We are in it together and together we will transform this world into a divine existence; full of love, co-operation, uniqueness, blissful happiness, contentment, abundance and peace

- This process starts and finishes with you

- The Beatles said 'Love is all there is'

- The truth is, all there is, is 'Love and the Light of Pure Awareness'

New Awakening Reiki and the Evolution of the New Awakening Process

The New Awakening Reiki system was the original process containing six beautiful courses which are complete in themselves. It is a beautiful energetic system created from the purity of Divine Love Presence. The New Awakening Process takes you one step further as it contains True-self enquiry. The complete process contains development courses for all the three stages of evolution that all human-beings go through.

Stage One is Personal Fulfilment

Reiki Healing First Degree

Creating Abundance for The Excellent You

Love and Relationships

Stage Two is Soul Evolution

Sat Guru Sacred Mantra Practice

Reiki Healing Second Degree

The Gateway to Enlightenment

Stage Three is True Self Awakening

Gentle Touch Practice

Reiki Master Teacher

The Lotus Sutra Practice

You can work through the New Awakening Process on your own or within a New Awakening Community.

The Lotus Sutra Mystical Practice

Chanting the Mantra whilst you are reading the book will Awaken the Buddha Consciousness of Eternal Truth

ISBN 978-0-9926644-2-8

Sat Guru CD

By
New Awakening Sacred Mantra Singing Group

The Seekers Guide for a New Awakening
Supporting the Oneness Process

Essential Teachings for Your Awakening

The Excellent You - Creating Abundance
How to get what you really want

Love and Relationships
Creating loving meaningful relationships

The Gateway to Enlightenment
Awakening to Universal Laws

A new awakening for a golden spiritual age is presented in this book with suggestions and explanations as to how this beautiful concept can be achieved.

In addition the book contains three courses, with audio tutorials in MP3 format. These provide the spiritual seeker essential teachings to accelerate the process of Awakening. When a person awakens there is normally a transformation period when illusion is dissolved. These courses contain divine truths therefore they will accelerate your transformation process.

The Seekers Guide Course Handbook
Contains Three Courses
Audio Course 6 CDs plus a Meditation CD
ISBN 978-0-9561159-7-3

Available from our website
www.naturallyyou.co.uk

New Awakening Reiki Healing

Reiki Healing First Degree

This Home Study Multimedia Course is all about Healing Yourself, Family, Friends, Pets and Plants

Home Study Material from our website Course Manual, Reiki Music CD, Audio Tutorials

Includes Spiritual Attunements

ISBN 978-0-9561159-4-2

Reiki Healing Second Degree

This Home Study Multimedia Course Teaches Three Sacred Reiki Symbols for Physical, Emotional, Mental, Soul and Spiritual Distant Healing

Course Manual, Reiki Music CD, and Tutorial Audio Course 3 CD set

Includes Spiritual Attunements

ISBN 978-0-9561159-5-9

The Reiki Master – Teacher

This Home Study Multimedia Course Teaches The Reiki Masters Symbol

The Divine Wisdom of the The Lotus Sutra

How to Teach Reiki Healing Transferring the Spiritual Attunements

Course Book Manual and Audio Tutorials.

Includes Spiritual Attunements

ISBN 978-0-9561159-2-8

The New Awakening Process

The Divine Message About You

Sacred Teachings Supporting all Faiths

Gentle Touch Awakening Practice

by

Robert Bourne

Naturally You
Publishing

The Gentle Touch Practice CD is contained in
The New Awakening Process download

It is also available on Spotify and Apple Music search
Gentle Touch Practice by Robert Bourne

visit our website at

www.new-awakening.com

CPSIA information can be obtained
at www.ICGtesting.com
Printed in the USA
BVHW081043250620
582308BV00014B/1241